Peter Ralston

CHENG HSIN

The Principles of Effortless Power

North Atlantic Books
Berkeley, California

ISBN 1-55643-048-5

Published by
North Atlantic Books
P.O. Box 12327
Berkeley, California 94712

Cover and book design by Paula Morrison.
Typeset in Palatino by Campaigne and Somit Typography.
Printed in the United States of America by Walsworth Publishing Co.

Cheng Hsin: The Principles of Effortless Power is sponsored by the Society for the Study of Native Arts and Sciences, a nonprofit educational corporation whose goals are to develop an educational and crosscultural perspective linking various scientific, social, and artistic fields; to nurture a holistic view of arts, sciences, humanities, and healing; and to publish and distribute literature on the relationship of mind, body, and nature.

Table of Contents

Foreword

The following statement originated from an interview done in 1978. It has been edited into a foreword to provide a background context for the origins and purpose of this book. It deals mostly with some of the experiences that allowed me to discover and formulate the principles of Cheng Hsin (which is the name given to the work that I do).

I first started martial arts in Singapore when I was nine, but at the time it was simply another form of play. I started Judo with some friends. I didn't really start getting serious about it until I was almost sixteen. In time, as I progressed, although I went to school and did other things, in a lot of ways I isolated myself from the rest of the world, and I studied martial arts. I studied them intensely. My point was never to believe something somebody said, to adopt some one else's structure or beliefs. My point was simply to be very good. As a teenager I wanted to be the best fighter in the world. I think that attitude was very important to my success. A lot of people want to learn something, and simply study from someone who tells them to do this and that, and that's legitimate. However, the teacher may not be accurate, and often is simply coming from what he has heard or learned or believes. In any case, I wanted to make the art mine. And in order for it to be mine, *I* had to have the ability. I had to discover and understand it. It didn't do me any good if somebody said something and I believed it; only if *I* understood it, only when it was my experience and ability, was it useful.

So I studied and got better than my peers. In every art that I studied, I was at the head of the class. I did that in a year or two, which is really very fast; it usually takes a decade to do that. I mastered certain physical principles, and then I started to understand: "If I'm really going to be the best, then obviously I've got to understand and become more powerful in a lot more than just physical competency." I didn't use the term then, but the real meaning behind what I was after was that it would take a real transformation in me to accomplish that. I mean, I had to change, and I really had to do it.

One day when I was a teenager, studying Kung Fu, I was driving with a classmate to class. On the car seat was a book I had never seen before, called the *Tao Te Ching*. I picked it up, opened it and started reading, just a few lines, and I asked: "What is this?" My friend answered: "Well, our teacher said that Kung Fu comes from there, but I don't understand it. It doesn't make sense to me." I started reading it and I dropped my jaw. It was something I felt really good about. I said: "This is fantastic! It's amazing!" I was eighteen years old and I had never seen anything like it before. I didn't have any reference points in which to understand the language, but I was very drawn to it. He said: "If you like it, take it. It doesn't do me any good." So I did. I read the whole thing several times. There were a few passages I didn't understand at all, but some of it I felt I had a grasp of. I really enjoyed it.

I continued to study the great writings. As a matter of fact, I got into Zen and the *Tao Te Ching* for the same reason: to further my study in martial arts. Then, by and by, it turned around and my martial arts furthered my study of *that*, of discovery. Essentially, I was into discovering the fundamental nature of my own event, and I just turned it around so that instead of understanding my own event for the sake of martial arts, I began to use martial art to study my event.

Around that time, I would go to classes and fight kung fu or karate people, black belts, and win but still feel like I lost. I would win and feel bad. Something wasn't right. The thing about it was that I was winning from natural ability. I was winning because I was stronger, quicker, more aggressive than somebody else, but I wasn't winning because I really understood anything about martial art. I wasn't winning out of an understanding of relationship, or from any personal transformation. It was just a relative thing. Somebody who was faster and stronger than me would have beaten me. It wasn't right.

Eventually, I came to study with Wong Chia Man, a Chinese martial arts master who became one of my main teachers. He was the softest teacher I'd ever seen at that point, and the most relaxed. I learned a lot from him and studied really hard. It was a lot closer, I could tell, to what I wanted. But still there was a lack of satisfaction.

Then I ran into a man who's a friend of mine now. He came to the Bay Area as a T'ai Chi artist, and, after looking around at all the T'ai Chi people and other martial artists in the Bay Area, decided that he didn't like any of them. I was teaching then, still very young at this time, teaching Kung Fu, T'ai Chi, and some other arts. We played one afternoon—which is to say, although it looks like fighting it's really playing. In this case, however, there was no intention of hurting or even particularly beating each other. It was done for the skill and the love involved in the relationship.

I walked out of there after playing with him and I felt the satisfaction that I had been looking for. I said to myself, "This is it! This is what has been missing." It wasn't even in words. It was something communicated about the real play and the real relationship. It was in that situation where I first learned to drop fear. Not the fear of getting hurt, but the fear of losing. It had never occurred to me. I fought so often, and out of a hundred blows exchanged with anybody, they would always hit me at least a few times, and I didn't like that. I wanted to be perfect. I didn't want any blows in and I was striving for that.

This time, however, I noticed that if I wasn't afraid of getting hit, or of winning or losing, that it was easy. I wouldn't get hit! That was the first time I was able to never get hit, 100%. Because I didn't care. What that did was open up my perception to what was really happening, because I didn't have any investment in it. So it was easy. I just saw a fist coming and I'd move. And I saw it all the time because I wasn't stuck on any one. I wasn't worried about it. When I get worried about it, I become afraid of losing. Then I get stuck somewhere and get hit. It's a beautiful secret. That's one of the things I like about this kind of thing, it's an exacting and tremendous feedback. When you get stuck, you get told you're stuck (by getting hit).

Although I had several Black Belts in different arts and had studied sword, staff, spear, fencing at the University, tournament judo, aikido and western boxing, around my early twenties I really started to isolate myself. So, I didn't accomplish any more "badges" of any kind. I didn't care about that anymore and I pulled myself away. I didn't care if anybody knew what I knew. However, I didn't realize at the time that later on this would create a gap between me and my communication to others.

Around that time I was living in a shack, studying. I had

given up teaching. I had taught for a while; even when I was a teenager I was teaching. It was something I was always drawn to—but again, it was so I could immerse myself even more in what I was doing. When I look back, I can see that there was an incredible amount of what people generally call discipline. I can only see it by looking back because then that was the only thing that I knew, and it was simply normal life for me. There was an incredible amount of time, concentration, and energy put into my study that most people never know. I worked day and night on it, not just physically, but through contemplation and writing. I did reams and reams of writing because it served me in my study. I wouldn't write to anybody in particular, or maybe to somebody, someday. I was writing what I learned day-to-day, insights and realizations about it all.

I would train a minimum of five hours a day physically, and then I would teach sometimes on top of that. And during the rest of the day, for example, my friend and I used to hang out all morning, perhaps six hours, practicing in the courtyard, studying and talking. Later I would write and contemplate. The good part about this isolation was the incredible amount of discipline, the incredible amount of concentration of energy, attention, focus, contemplation, and involvement with my work. That's what made it, in one way. While I was doing that I didn't notice that it was anything not to be done. That was just simply what I did.

One day I was sitting in my backyard and a man came up to me. He had run into somebody who knew me. He said that he would like me to teach him martial arts. I told him that I wasn't doing that any more, but he was really persistent, so I began to teach again. Later he said he really wanted me to do some intensive contemplation work. I was twenty-one. He said, "I can see that you are ready and I really want you to do this." I said no. I couldn't see how anything significant could be brought about in only three days of intensive contemplation.

Later, however, I did it. This one was a five-day contemplation intensive held in Santa Rosa. I sat right down the first day, working on "Who am I", and on the first day, the first exercise, what I was getting was just blowing me away. I didn't have a direct experience of the truth right then, but went right into phenomenal experiences. The room started changing, it got bright, I saw colors, and the sense of myself was quite different, I felt expanded somehow.

This had never happened to me before. A whole different thing started to happen. Just working on this question.

At the end of five days, I felt more joy than I had ever felt in my life! I was really happy. I hadn't noticed that I hadn't been. So, I was absolutely sold on this kind of work. It was beautiful. Two weeks later, I went up to a place in the mountains and did my second Intensive, working on "What am I?"

I spent the entire time very willfully and very dynamically, going for a direct experience of what I am. I threw everything I had into it for three days solid, every moment. I didn't let up. I didn't notice I let up, anyway. I did it like I did most other things, with just so much drive, so much energy, so much attention in every moment. Thinking back about that, I don't know if I could do it like that anymore.

But I didn't get it. I didn't directly experience what I am. I didn't have an enlightenment experience. It had never occurred to me that I wouldn't. I thought that I *never* failed at these things! Three days and I didn't get a direct experience of the nature of my own Being: "It can *not* happen!" It didn't even dawn on me that it might not happen. I felt like I received tremendous value out of it anyway, and I was sitting around and doing incredible things at a celebration afterwards. I felt as though I could turn my body-awareness inside out and become the music that was being played.

I had come up with the man who first invited me to do this kind of work, and I had to wait to take a ride with him. We stayed overnight and hung around the next day. It was really nice, we were in no hurry. He was talking with some people, and so I read *Jonathan Livingston Seagull*. I just found it up there and I read it that morning. I was hanging out doing things like sitting at the top of a ladder, trying to get to the bottom without moving my body. I was trying to do the Livingston Seagull thing, right? I was really trying to do it! I still didn't believe that I couldn't do *anything*.

Late that afternoon, I was sitting up against a wall in an L-shaped room. Some people were around the corner talking. I was just sitting there feeling good, not doing anything, not contemplating in particular, and I had an enlightenment experience on what I am. It was a major breakthrough, the nature of which was completely outside of previous experience. It was somehow outside of "experience" and, at the same time, absolutely transformed my experience. It was profoundly and perfectly the case. I prefer to say it "dawned" on me. I like that word, "dawned." It changed my whole life and the structure in which I held reality. It was fabulous!

Suddenly, I was aware that I was Nothing. Absolutely no thing. I directly experienced my true nature, not as thingness in any way, shape or form. The possibility that I wasn't *any*thing had not existed for me. Through the whole Intensive I was every thing, every conceptualization, every movement, every effort. It never occurred to me that I wasn't anything. In the enlightenment I was just . . . no thing, no where, no substance whatsoever. It was the first and probably the most significant enlightenment experience I ever had, although I had several others later. Because it was the first, I consider it is probably the most significant. No intellectual understanding of the matter can ever come close to a direct enlightenment.

One week later, sitting at home, I had an enlightenment experience on the nature of another. I became conscious that others are exactly the same as what I am. I'm nothing and occupy no space, no location, and given they don't occupy a location and I don't occupy a location, then we're *not separate*! And that was a mind blower. That we are really not separate. We are the same one!

It was after those enlightenment experiences that abilities like being able to read somebody's disposition accurately started to come. I was able to see what people were going to do before they did it. So, when somebody was going to hit me, I would finish the situation before they were able to, and that was it.

Sometimes in class people would ask, "How would you deal with a situation where someone is going to hit you?" I'd say, "Hit me." And the moment they would think to hit me and start to motivate their body, I'd stop them. That's it. Handled. I suppose in one sense you could say I noticed their mind. I was seeing where they were coming from, the source of where the action arose. Seeing the bottom of the motivation of their thought and actions through knowing what I am and what they are. I knew where they were coming from and would watch them spring from there: that appeared to me, not visually, but that touched me before their body moved. If it's a process for them in which they have to manifest into thought, and then into action, I can act before they arrive at their action.

I just was dealing with the situation in a more real sense. I was dealing with what was true, and that ability happened because it is aligned to what is true. I didn't notice that that ability was something I could develop, or was something that somebody didn't have but could develop. At that time, Cheng Hsin was still on the horizon, and I was just beginning to clarify what was later to be known as the Principles of Being, alignment to which allows for great functional capacity.

One of the things that happened in that period of time was that I got so good at this that I wasn't able to play any more. I just kept finishing everything before it got started. And, in a funny sense that threatened me. I didn't feel that I had completed my studies of everything there was to learn about martial arts, or all of the principles involved, and other possibilities, different powers, methods, movements and cultivations. Yet, if I continued to intercede like this, I wasn't going to learn anything new. I had destroyed the game. So, what I had to do was tie one hand behind my back, so to speak, and go again. I simply stopped using that ability for awhile.

Martial arts, or being good at fighting, was the game that I was invested in. The "stuff" that I attached myself to. My makeup had a lot to do with martial arts at that time, and who I was . . . not in the enlightenment sense, but who I was in the common usage of that word. So, I had a lot of personal investment in keeping the game, especially because I didn't feel like I was finished with it.

Sometime later I did a Fourteen-Day Intensive led by Charles Berner. A lot of interesting people and a lot of "old hands" were there. Werner Erhard was there. It was incredibly tough sometimes, and yet it was very powerful. On the fourteenth day, I hadn't gotten it. I was working on "What is Life?" or more accurately, "What is Existence?" I was working with Neil Goldberg at the time and, on the last exercise of the last day, during the last ten minutes, I had an enlightenment experience. The first enlightenment experience I had was the most significant, but this one was the most profound.

It was the last exercise, and if I hadn't gotten it in fourteen days what difference could this one exercise make? So, I was just enjoying myself. I was sitting across from Neil and was playing. For some unknown reason I decided to go up out the top of my head, a distance that felt like a few feet above my head. It felt like I would go up there and meet Neil, like we joined up there. And then, quite to my surprise, I had an experience of what the Zen people call the Void. That Absolute Existence does not exist. There was no distance, no time, no space . . . nothing.

I guess my appearance changed dramatically at the time, since, after we were done with the exercise, Neil was jumping up and down pointing, saying, "You should look in a mirror!" Exclaiming how different my face looked.

Anyway, when I got home there was a full-length mirror. I hadn't looked in a mirror for fourteen days. I walked up to the mirror and looked at myself and it was a deep shock to my body. It was a shock because I saw a body that I had known before, and it wasn't me! Not that my appearance had changed. The similarity is what shocked me. In some sense I had forgotten that I had a body. It's like the body reflected my history, my character, my ideas, my personality, all the things I thought I was. All the things I had been being. Without thinking about it, I really expected my reflection *not* to have shown up.

I recognize now that I didn't have a context in which to hold that experience. I had experienced the Absolute Nature of existence, yet when I was back in "life," I just noticed that everybody lied. That everything said and everything done was a lie. It was not the Truth. And it started to become intolerable. Then I noticed that everything I said was a lie. That I wasn't able to speak the Truth. I started to go crazy, so I isolated myself for two weeks and wouldn't speak. I didn't know what to do with it. I think it is invaluable to have a context in which to hold such an enlightenment experience.

New abilities started to arise. I told you of the ability to read someone before they moved. This one started to arise: I didn't have to be cognizant of any movement on their part, psychic or otherwise, to know what to do. I just knew. That blew me away. I didn't have to perceive a thing. The other ability was perceiving the beginning. With this I wasn't perceiving anything!

I started to notice that I would do something and would ask myself "Why did I do that?" Then I would see it was appropriate. I would start to move and then someone would throw a kick or punch and I was moving out of the way of their action, but I was doing it before I even knew why. I just moved and they would throw a kick and miss and I'd think, "If I'm moving before I know what they're going to do, how do I know if they're going to move this way or that way? What if I move and it's inappropriate?" Then I started to notice that I kept doing it appropriately. I would move, but I had no idea why. My body would move. It was like I didn't make the decision actually—and would see my body moving and say, "What are you doing, body?" And then a fist would come, "Whooosh!" from behind me and I didn't even see it. That's really interesting. And very simple, very simple.

After all of that, winning the World Championship was easy. I did that because . . . well, for one thing, I had given up martial arts in a sense, and I'd never been recognized for what I'd accomplished. I knew I was good. This World Tournament was the second and maybe the last. In 1928, in mainland China, the first big tournament was held. It was very dangerous, lots of people were killed or injured. They finally stopped the 1928 Nanking Tournament at the last thirteen people because they didn't want them to kill themselves off. From that time on there have been others—for a time there was the tradition of having them every year, and it was called the Asian Martial Arts tournament, and throughout the entire period I suppose anybody could have entered. Finally, they called it the World Tournament and invited all countries to participate. When I was there, there were Japanese, Thais, French, Saudi Arabians, Australians, other people from the United States and many other countries, but most were Chinese and it was usually won by Chinese. This was the first time that a non-Asian had ever won.

I did it for two reasons. It was to complete something for me, and to begin something new. Now the completion part of it was that I was no longer going to be involved with that part of martial arts, and I wanted a little recognition. One of the fundamental reasons that I did it is that I'm quite radically different in the world of martial arts; I ask people to do very "uncommon" things, to take on apparently unrelated inquiries, and I demand a very deep level of understanding. I want people to listen to me, to open up to what I'm saying. Winning this World tournament was done so that I could say: "I did it. What I'm teaching you is functional. It works." Now they'll consider it. People listen to me now who wouldn't before, yet I'm saying the same thing.

I knew some time before the tournament that martial arts the way I knew them was coming to a close for me. My playing the game of learning it and mastering it was coming to a close. There was no place I could go. In 1975 I traveled around the world. I traveled to all sorts of countries and looked. I looked at masters and teachers, all over countries in Asia, and there was nobody I wanted to study with. So, I had in one sense given up martial arts before I even did the World Championship.

I decided that if I were to continue to do this, I wanted to do some other things. I wanted to start contributing what I did and what I knew in a much larger way. I wanted to transform the martial arts in the world. Which is saying a hell of a lot, because even to change people's view of what that is would be phenomenal. And I started to consider, "What if people could get . . . what contention is."

One time I came up with a phrase. This was around 1973. I was standing out in my backyard in the pine trees. I had walked out there, and I had a sense that somebody was around. It was very dark, and I had some apprehension. I wondered: "Am I going to have to fight somebody, a burglar or something"? As I was standing there in the yard, I truly opened up to the possibility of that event, and suddenly everything became safe. I guess that's the only way I could say it. The realization was at the time—what I said out loud into the yard was: *"There is no such thing as a fight, there never was and there never will be."*

This level of understanding is very difficult to reach without some ontological work (by that I mean contemplative or in-depth considerations into the nature of "Being"). So the first thing it occurred to me to get across was that even when people are fighting, they at least have to do it in relationship. People just didn't understand that. It's just all very simple. I don't do anything in particular, I simply establish an appropriate and responsive relationship with the opponent in every moment. I have had martial artists—so-called martial artists, Kung Fu people, boxers, Karate people, internal martial artists and others—come and play with me and say, "Hey, you're really good," and I think: it's not good, it's just simple! And they simply don't understand.

So, they come to me and want to know what this is. But most martial artists can't stand me for too long because they ask me to teach them how to be good, and when I go about doing that, it's unacceptable to them.

One thing I started to notice was that my understanding in martial arts and other things that I do in my pursuit . . . see, I don't like calling it "martial arts" any more because it's so much more than that . . . but in what I do, was not being reflected in the rest of my life to the degree it was in my work. So, I started to change that around, to look at that, and approach things differently. It's been difficult. So, when I stopped isolating myself, it was a whole other kettle of fish. I found that to deal with one's entire relationship to life is *the* most demanding endeavor. Yet I discovered that the things that come up between people—events and so-called "problems"—are really a parallel to what occurs in martial interaction and in fighting. However, translation from one domain to the next is not easy. It requires a fundamental experience of the principles involved such that they can be recognized in any form. And it also requires a training ground, the purpose of which is to transform the very body and being of the individual into alignment with those principles. So it is that Shissai (a master "Zen" swordsman, Japan, 1728) said:

> Thus it is important to teach men how to acquire discretion, great insight, forthright conviction, and an honest Heart. To teach them to acquire a personal awareness and self-discipline and thereby place them on the solid ground of practice.

Cheng Hsin offers that solid ground.

It has a lot to do with rearranging the patterns and design of our body, thinking, feeling and perceptions. Cheng Hsin is a total endeavor, requiring a transformation of the entire Being, not just one aspect. We already appear as a multi-dimensional event, and any powerful and ultimately effective study or practice must address itself to that fact.

I would like to see martial arts turned into a place for the development of human beings, and of honesty. A place where we can see what it is that we do in life that really makes us suffer and hurt, or be ineffective and incomplete. Martial arts is an excellent place to see that, if it is done right. Otherwise—and 99% of the time it *is* otherwise—it is done like everything else, just to add to our survival and protection, our "rightness," and this ends up increasing resistance and separation—it's the same approach we have to everything else. I'd like to see it become as functional as it can be. A very valuable tool, the way of a Warrior, not the way of pretense and struggle. Really use it as a tool for growth, not self-deceit.

I would also like to make it available to many more people. I work with groups, organizations, classes, and people privately. What I would really like to do is put it out to different kinds of people. Often people who get into martial arts are coming from a particular way of thinking, looking for something specific. I'd like to put it out for people who'd really like something they can do to give them immediate and accurate feedback on the nature of their consciousness. People who want a place that offers a real study into the nature of their own event. People who are willing to be confronted with the truth and take on an experiential understanding and transformation of the event of Being that we are, bodily, mentally, psychically, and beyond. And people willing to be honest with themselves. I just have the sense that if more of those people could hear what I want to do, they would be interested. They would be excited about it.

When the words "martial arts" are mentioned, people generally think of something very crude or limited; that is why I say I don't do that. Cheng Hsin is so much more than that. However, when a friend of mine was talking to a publisher of a "consciousness" magazine and made mention of consciousness in fighting, his response was, "What does fighting have to do with consciousness?" I'd like to answer that question.

Introduction, or "How to Read this Book"

So often we use information, or view communication, as simply a means to check up on or verify what we already believe or know or have heard. The opportunity held by being in relationship to this work is not to see how it fits in with where we're at, but to use such a relationship to go beyond where we are; to extend our understanding, dissolve our beliefs, and transform the limitations that we have adopted. Every single sentence in this book is an opportunity to do that. It is not something that can be read like a novel or an instruction manual; it must be studied, contemplated, and experienced. You must look into your own case, and open it up.

I never learned anything that I already 'knew.'

No matter how many times you read this (and it should be read many times), it will never appear the same. The book will seem to change as you change. When, years after your initial confrontation with the communication held within, you happen to be moved into new realms of being, if you pick it up again you will find that it speaks to the depth that you presently experience.

This book was written over a period of seven years, and some material in it dates back to 1971. Some of the content tends to be more simply stated, and some is set up to demand more contemplation and depth of consideration before anything becomes truly clear or useful.

Very much may be said in very little, so take care not to bypass the implications of something stated simply. Remember, we are studying to experience the freedom and integrity found naturally in an understanding of Being. The purpose of teaching Cheng Hsin is to communicate an experience of Being at its source; further, it is to empower an adaptation to this position. This will arise as a way of being, one that is fully creative and recognized as created, aligned to the truth of things, and oriented to the openess and unlimited nature that is Being. When Cheng Hsin is fully realized, this "way" of being naturally arises and the communication of what was the Teaching springs up as qualities that simply reflect this integrity of Being.

> *Only the 'form' survives of anything created and then passed on in time since the creativity lay in the formless (source) and this formlessness cannot survive, having never existed. Therefore, only when the form is being consciously used or created in this moment is it truly useful. Otherwise it is hollow and useless, simply a binding force, a limitation.*

I hope you have as profound an experience each time you read this as I had in writing it.

Peter Ralston

Chapter One

The Principles of Cheng Hsin

C heng Hsin is the source or origin of what I call the Principles of Being. By its very nature Cheng Hsin will always remain elusive and ungraspable. Know that you must look past the words and even past your thoughts and feelings to comprehend it (but not past what's actually true in your present experience).

> *Cheng Hsin is the Prior Nature of Being, the Integrity of Being, and the Source of Being.*

Although there is not much else to say about it, I want to give you a more solid ground from which to approach this work, and therefore I have written the rest of this book.

I'll begin with definitions and translations of the words. *Cheng* can be defined as *principle, true, genuine, real, right, correct,* or *exact. Hsin* is often defined as *heart, mind, will, sense, center, origin,* or *source.* Together they have been translated in many ways. Taoist and Zen traditions use the word *Hsin* to refer to "one's true nature." It is the seat of Being, the primary nature and reality of consciousness and life, the origin of self.

Essentially, *Hsin* refers to the source and union between being alive or an entity and being a body or an objective form. There is a source that creates all that is the event of being; this is *Hsin.* Since *Hsin* is the origin, it is also the union. In practical or useful terms, the word "Being" provides us the simplest approach to understanding Cheng Hsin via the English language. However, we must consider that what we are speaking about is the origin of being as well as its substance and nature. This is paradoxical.

1

It is Cheng Hsin.

It is simply as it is.

The basic principle of Cheng Hsin as it occurs in the event of Being, (being a body, being alive and in interaction) is presented and approached through several apparently separate considerations. Practically speaking, this form of presentation is much easier to grasp, since it is especially difficult to realize the actual principle of Cheng Hsin itself. To discover what the One Principle is, behind the subprinciples that we use to study it, is possible, profound, and encouraged. I sometimes refer to Cheng Hsin as the *Integrity of Being.* This phrase is meant to be heard as all of the possible meanings the word "integrity" encompasses.

Sometimes I've found it is best to leave a communication in a slightly obscure form without attempting to elucidate it into "practical" terms, so that the reader or hearer is forced to seek out for himself the experience inherent in it. Of course, this approach is not intended to obscure the experience, or make it difficult to reach. It is meant to maximize an experiential encounter, and the subject is actually elucidated as much as possible. What follows is an attempt to outline these fundamental principles.

When we take on a task such as experiencing, learning and adapting to the fundamental nature of Being, we need to begin by looking at what is most primary and present. Therefore, we look at the body-being. This is simply what appears "to" and "as" us when Being appears as a thing. This includes the presence of body, feelings, and thoughts. Generally, our body-being is all that constitutes our conventional sense of being a living entity. In the study and observation of this way of being and its design, it is possible to notice some very basic principles that arise in relationship to the experience or expression of this aspect of Being. These are the Principles of Body-Being, which appear or spring from Cheng Hsin. Whatever they are, regardless of what is said about them, the principles are useful only when experienced. And this can only be done by beginning with where we presently stand, and what we actually experience as being. We need to tell the truth.

To further this right now, do not deny any aspect of yourself, good or bad. Look at the way you are now, for it is the only way to begin. Ten years from now it will still be the only way to begin.

All that you think is 'you,' is an interpretation. Don't overlook the raw and mundane—it is this. What is really going on? What are you always doing? This is the real pursuit and source of this study.

At this moment, just as you sit or stand, get a sense of yourself. Don't withhold anything from yourself about yourself. Now, feel as if you are not withholding anything about you from anyone else. This is the creative source you must work with, the acknowledgement and awareness of which will accelerate your progress greatly. If you didn't get a real sense of this, put this book down, and contemplate until you do. I'll wait.

The Five Principles of Body-Being

In order to further our experimentation and investigation of the Principle that I refer to "as" Cheng Hsin and as springing "from" Cheng Hsin, I have made some distinctions within that which appears as Being. The first distinction is that Being appears first and foremost as some "thing" that is, in our case a body-being. What appears to be true about Being as a body is that bodily existence is formed out of the principles that give it design and allows for it to "be." This can be seen as the principle or principles in which Being exists as a thing. I divide this principle into five parts, and then speak about the state or occurrence that seems to arise from it, which is to say, from alignment of the body-being with the principle. I refer to this as the "Five-Word Principle."

The Five Cheng Hsin Principles of Body-Being:

1. Being calm
2. Relaxing
3. Centering
4. Grounding
5. Being whole and total

Actually, the words act only as a reference and are not the principle itself. As a matter of fact, they do not really indicate what the principle is; it is perhaps more accurate to say that they refer to what arises out of being aligned to the principle. When the event of Being occurs in alignment with any principle that founds the condition in which being exists, the state "in" which and "of" which being is abiding shifts to its most fundamental position, which is also its most workable condition. This implies that it is possible to fall out of alignment with the very principles that found the event that *is* falling out of alignment. Yet it also indicates that the principles are in effect whether we are in alignment with them or not.

As an example of this, consider a hose. The hose has a particular design and function. Certain principles determine its design. Yet the hose can be twisted such that it does not fulfill its function. In this case we cannot say that the principles have changed at all, yet the state of the hose is quite different from when it is allowed to function as it was designed to. Through activities such as negation, confusion, resistance, abstraction, ignorance, suppression, lying, and the like, it is possible for the principles that found any event or being to be in discord. In other words, it is not allowed to function or "be" simply as it is designed to be. The activity will then arise from an aberration of the principle and not from the principle in its pure and most powerful form.

> *Natural principle is simply adherence to the form of Being in this moment. The principles, or the occasion of consciousness that we are all attached to or identified with within limitation, are the demands of life. We must first follow the demands of life, or event, to arise into it without conflict. The more consciously this is done, the more power or fullness and creativity our participation in Being will have. Once we actively join its movement, we are free to create.*

When alignment occurs with any particular principle, the original state of being appears in relationship to that principle. The five principles of body-being, or of being a body, are the state or condition that arises out of an alignment with the fundamental principles that comprise what I call "being human like a thing." I will refer to the principle itself, without really naming it, within the description of the state of being that appears in the principle's unfettered presence.

1. BEING CALM—THE PRESENCE OF BEING

Sometimes we experience a state that we call "being calm." How this comes about is fundamentally unknown to us; however, we suspect that it is due to some sort of control on our part, and so we take credit for it. It is conventionally attributed to "mind" control. It is thought of as a state of mind in which the activity of mind is clear, at ease, and undisturbed. When I speak of calming the activity that we call "mind," it is not to support the manifold assumptions that exist as mind, but to point to a principle that appears in the presence of what we're calling Calm. Being calm appears as the state that *is,* when our internal activity is aligned to the principle of being for which this is so. The principle seems tied to the presence of being, in which the mere presence of being is allowed to be, regardless of how it appears. Being is experienced without preference or aversion, no matter the form.

When the activity or function that occurs as mind is distorted into a form or function in which that activity appears to be disturbed or unsettled, it is often rejected and held as something wrong, something to be avoided. This relationship to what is apparently already occurring immediately severs us from the activity itself, putting us in the position of "fixer" rather than "doer," or simply being. This occurs the moment we first ascertain that we are not calm. From this position we are not in the place that can correct this malady, should we hold that it needs fixing, and so a struggle ensues to move to or find the place in which the disturbance can be corrected. This way of holding calm makes calm almost inaccessible.

Being calm is essential to all that we do. Having a calm mind doesn't depend on appearance. It doesn't depend on situations. It is more powerful to see calmness not as something that we have to make or force into being, but as something already existing or simply as a quality of being in which we can abide, something to be fallen into or uncovered. It can be held as a root or context to those qualities that we call not-calm, or different from calm. Thus we can see calmness not as something that we do, like jumping from item to item, but as a shift into the sea in which all things float.

> *It is the tendency to movement that exercises and shows to consciousness the power of stillness in Being.*

We have a tendency to get caught up in things that don't serve being "in" or being responsive to the present moment and condition; we become enmeshed in figuring out, being anxious, upset, angry, fearful, reactive, and so on. By holding calm in the way that I've suggested, we can simply not "do" those things. It will be more useful to regard this as a shift to that which is not bound to any item and also not exclusive of them. Then, instead of trying to make those things disappear, we can simply let them be, not feed them energy and attention, and let them float in the base that we now call being calm. It is from this principle that we can be responsive and clear.

> *Recognize that stillness of Being is not contrary to the activity of life.*

Our immediate endeavor in following Principle One is to calm the mind and use only the presence of Being to direct our actions. We must trust the dictates of our calm presence rather than our body's strength, or emotional excitement.

I began to speak about these principles in the early '70s. At that time I happened to write a letter to a student who had moved. I want to quote from the letter and provide an older and different form of expression of these principles:

> Calm your mind and control it. Control it by letting it be (empty). Also your heart. With true presence one will yield to but also stick to activity. In the midst of movements, force and emotional excitement, control and calm your mind so that you may follow activity unhampered and unchanged.

What we do with our mind is very important, so we must study that activity. Being controls the body. It also controls thoughts, emotions, and the energy of the body. However, most of us are controlled by and identified with mind, and so mind influences and appears to control everything we do. We will have a hard time if we try to deal with the body or some other aspect like emotion alone, since it is being governed or influenced by contributing forces. Trying to work with the body state alone, say, to relax and be centered, *is* working with mind.

By working with the motivating habitual assumptions of "being" that permeate your living and actions, you can make transformative changes in the body. Simply to control the body inside and out is generally considered a mind function, and so not controlling the mind creates difficulty in directing the body. As an analogy: if your gas stove catches on fire it is difficult to try and blow out the flame. Even if this puts out the fire, another spark will immediately set it off again. Better to turn off the gas! So it is with the source of mind. Every other principle and all that you do starts here. If you want to relax, this is how you do it. Do you want to move this, turn from here, sink that, feel this? You must direct these things. This is the beginning of "mind-power." Every single thing that you do is done with the "force of your Being" or the "force of being alive,"—what we could call "life force"—and so it is with mind. Get nearer to the root of your mind and you get nearer to the source of the doing.

> *The moon reflects in still water clearly. In moving water, although the appearance is different, the moon is still the same. Knowing this one stills the mind even in motion. In stillness there is always potential for action. Know the nature of the water and the moon, no matter the condition.*

2. RELAXING

If I had to choose a single principle to follow, it would probably be the principle that manifests itself as the state of being relaxed. Taken at its broadest meaning, this principle permeates every aspect of what we do. The principle here seems to evoke being at rest, or the "unused state." It is what is so about anything before self's activity uses the thing for a purpose other than simply being and performing its natural function. Therefore our alignment to this principle requires us to remain and/or to return constantly to the unused or open state, the position of rest or natural function: allowing things to "sit on the floor" rather than "holding them up." To relax we must actually endeavor to make all of our tissues completely supple, even limp. None of our joints should be locked. We must direct this, and feel the body loosen and open. When we move, using relaxation as our principle, it will not feel like ordinary movement.

Again, from the same letter:

> Relax; let all your joints fall open and your tissues be supple and loose. Let everything go (down to the feet). Use the inherent binding force of your tissues, regardless of how relaxed they are, to connect your body. Use gravity as your primary force, and the earth as your prime principle and closest ally.

The only way you can use gravity as your source of movement is to relax. You must relax into the earth rather than resist it. No matter how relaxed you become, relax more! Don't worry, your body won't go anywhere. If it is as relaxed as water it will still be together—a lump on the floor perhaps, but together. Rest assured: no matter how relaxed your body becomes, you can always tense up again. True relaxing can be a slow process, but don't put it off. Relax now, totally, unconditionally.

You must surrender your mind to relax—even the notion that you have a mind. Above all, let go of any separation of that activity from bodily impulse. Feel yourself letting go so that your body isn't "held" so much, nor your mind, nor your energy. When you relax your tissues, blood, organs, the muscles around your organs, *everything*, then the energy will flow. It is this very relaxation that allows for the ch'i, or energy inherent in your body-being, to circulate, develop, and be used. As Cheng said: "Throw open your entire body; let the ch'i flow without obstacle."

William Chen tells a story of a man who studied T'ai Chi for thirty years, insisting that he was relaxed. Whenever they had a match, William beat him soundly. The fellow asked why, and William told him that it was because he was not relaxed. Insisting that he was, this man went on denying his real state, and never relaxing. One can spend a whole lifetime denying aspects about oneself. Most of us do. However, this merely postpones immediate suffering, and allows for no growth. This man obviously had a limited sense of what relaxing meant, or denied that he was not relaxing—probably both.

If a problem seems to arise because you relax, you can trace it to an inability to do something else. For example, if upon relaxing your arm to someone's aggression he hits your body, it's not because you relaxed your arm but because you did not move your body! Many teachers say "relax," and follow it with "but." I will not.

> To 'relax under fire' means to stay calm and relaxed even in stressful situations. This reveals the true strength of your position, and thus the appropriate change.

It has been demonstrated that deep muscular relaxation cannot coexist with anxiety. Where there is one there cannot be the other. A calm mind seems to be the outcome of relaxing in this manner, as well as a supple and free body.

Looseness allows freedom of movement and change. It also permits a spontaneous response to force and activity in a manner that cannot be accomplished in any other way. Relaxation allows for greater speed, changeability, effortless power, balance, and more skill than can be conceived by following any other method, and is necessary in order to accomplish all of the other principles. Through relaxing we not only have a supple body, but we've calmed our mind in the process, and have freed our energy. Freeing all of our energy, or body-feeling, is the only real way to unify our whole body. Since gravity is a constant force, the freed energy and relaxed tissues will naturally go down, so the process of sinking begins here as well. Relaxing is profoundly beneficial in opening our sensitivities, awareness, listening and receiving energy, and what it does for our skills and abilities is tremendous. I will speak about these aspects later in the book, but none of them can be realized without this very essential state called relaxing.

3. CENTERING

We often forget that there is more intelligence arising as our body-being than just our mental facility (that which we most frequently refer to as "intelligence"). Actually, we find a real intelligence appearing as the "heart" and also as the "center." In the body, the center finds location in the lower abdomen. This center intelligence is most profound. It is not like the head intelligence, but then neither is the heart. It is here in the center region that we would keep our attention, thus calming and controlling it by that very act.

Centering is perhaps the best way to calm our intellect and emotions. Putting attention and feeling in the center region of the body allows a shift in state of being to one that is calm, non-thinking, balanced, aware, in-the-body, grounded, present, and alive. It also coordinates and harmonizes all movement in the body. All actions and movements are done with more power and control when directed by and coming from the center.

In physics, it is clear that the center of mass is the governing point for the movement of the mass. Adjusting the center of our body-mass is the most effective way to adjust its whole structure, including its balance, location, and direction, and the relationship of all its parts to one another. Hence it is the center that controls the power and integrity of the body. When we hold attention/awareness in the center part of the body, one spot below the navel in the abdomen, our attention, feeling, motivation, and intuitive understanding are a great deal more functional and effective than before we became centered. So we deliberately position being as attention-awareness in the center region.

Throughout history, this one area of concentration has become famous in martial arts and other arts of power and relationship. This region is a seat of power in human beings. Abiding here simplifies our relationship to the world, so that we see it much more clearly. The mind as thought does not interfere and confuse the issue, because the mind as thought does not exist when the attention is completely put on the center region. All that remains is a very direct relationship with our body-being and external existence. At this stage, any separation between these two (our body and other-than-our-body) lies only in appearance, and not in consideration, nor do they appear disconnected in any way. Centering calms the mind, making it clear and powerful, unquestioning and unknowing, and reveals the source and direction of action, spontaneously and without process.

We begin by getting in touch with the center region on a physical level. Then we move our whole body, our limbs and our entire mass, from that place. Whether turning or moving to or fro, that spot *is* the movement. If we want to move forward, the center moves forward and our body follows. If we want to move backwards or turn to the left or right, it is the sphere in the center that turns, moves, or twists, and the body follows. When the "mind" that abides in the center directs movement, the body follows. If all movements are completely centered, alignments and balance will naturally fall into place.

There are aspects of this field of study that are sometimes emphasized or made pivotal to the rest of the aspects in consideration. Centering is one of those. Indeed, it would be possible to devise an entire art founded totally and solely upon this one point. Many cults, warrior trainings, esoteric and metaphysical techniques revolve around this one principle of centering. It is possible through the concentration on this one spot to get in touch with power on many real, direct, and psychic levels. In physical relationship it moves the body as a whole and allows it to be directed effectively, yet its value does not stop there; centering is also important in what it does for our energy and mind.

In my life, I have often spent time intensely concentrating on that spot, and have a great deal of practice moving from there. It is my experience that this produces tremendous results. It was one of my main points of concentration in fighting in the World Tournament and has served me greatly.

The center region is concentrated in a place within the abdomen. You should feel this place to be large enough to be powerful and yet not so large that you cannot maintain its density. Performing any functional activity while concentrating on that spot automatically increases the power, skill, and effectiveness of that activity. The relationship between the whole body and the center should be investigated. They are inseparable; without one there is no other. Merely knowing this does little; the principles involved and the unifying, or contextual, principle from which they spring need to be experienced and understood in one's own Being.

Purpose and intelligence of purpose should spring from the center. The center is the abode of the "intelligence" that directly engages activity and responds to it spontaneously and with accuracy. However, this intelligence does not channel through a process of intellectual considerations, solving, knowing, remembering, or thinking. It is direct and answers directly.

Use a calm mind unhampered by external influence.

"Center mind" is a source of determination in both senses of that word: to be "determined" or deliberate; and "to determine," as in directing and choosing, or knowing what to choose. When our attention abides in the center region, and we surrender our "intellect" to the power of that act, then we are given a connection with intuitive intelligence. This intelligence will tell us what is appropriate, or what to do in this moment and situation, if we simply listen to it. Its communication is direct, simple, and usually comes in a feeling or in a non-thinking form.

4. GROUNDING (Sinking)

In our culture the word "sinking" does not have the same associations as "grounding." Therefore, I'm using the word "grounding" as well as "sinking" to refer to the state that is established by aligning to the principle that, for us, appears primarily as a powerful relationship with the earth. First of all, the basis of the word "grounding" is the "ground," which is what we want to "sink" into. "Grounding" in electrical terms, which does not entail sinking, is also applicable to our practice. To sink implies to lower into, to move downward, and this is also inherent to this principle.

Sinking begins by relaxing the muscles, letting them drop to a lower position (weight tending down). This process allows access to intrinsic strength (by unlocking joints and disengaging bones), and increases energy circulation. Relaxation allows tissues, breath, blood, and consciousness to sink. When this occurs you will also feel a sinking down toward the center region. As you step, it is the weighted leg that relaxes—"falls," if you will—and this fall transfers to press the other foot; as this occurs, sink your breath.

Whether moving or standing still, you must carry the upper body literally resting on the pelvis and legs. You should feel this to be so. The chest, shoulders, belly, arms, et al. just relax, and their entire weight is carried by the legs. The legs must also relax and support this body like a rubber ball would support it, catching it into the earth, not pushing it away. One leg is empty (slightly compressed) and relaxed; the other, full (more compressed) but still relaxed! You must loosen the pelvis so that the energy can sink down into the legs and feet, and accept the weight. If you relax and sink when standing mostly on one leg, that leg will feel as if it is carrying a great deal more weight than usual, and that foot will feel an increase in the pressure against the earth.

Continuing with the letter:

> Drop your attention, and massive feeling-energy (the feeling sense of the body-being), to the earth. Let more than relaxed tissues weight you into the earth. Feel and lower your attention, energy, sense of being and awareness to your center, to your feet, and into the earth, so that you indeed feel as if you are much closer to and in relationship with the earth, and much lower in your body. When your hand goes up, or any other part (your foot, shoulder, knee, elbow, head, etc.), every part of the body stays relaxed, and your energy does not go up; your attention and feeling stay down, sunk in the earth! The ch'i will expand by itself just in the act of lifting a hand, if your mind stays down in the lower extremities, the ch'i hugs the earth, and the body is very relaxed. When moving, maintain this state and true power, balance and stability will be yours.

I further commented on the finding and sinking of the ch'i (life force):

> Dwell on your 'sense of being' to know ch'i. Once you have a strong sense of your own Being (without looking at or thinking about it) you are right on top of ch'i. The intuitive movement that really cannot be separated from your 'mind'

and sense of being is the life force. When you move your sense of being down, and feel and concentrate on the lower parts (such as the pelvis, legs, feet, and ground), your energy will follow. To move your life force, your mind cannot be abstract or just intellect; it must be in your body, 'locked-together,' so that a thought is a bodily function. Then your energy will move with your mind. If you want to move all life force, unified, then move your entire sense of being, every part of yourself, together! Move all of your mind so that no thought or attention is separate from the actual sense of being that you are sinking into the earth, center and legs. This is sinking, or moving your energy. If you collect it all *en masse*, by feeling your totality, then it is powerful.

Sinking is not just a mental or physical affair; it is also emotional. Besides the specific energy that moves down, attitudes and emotions are engaged or activated as a result of this movement. A sense of surrendering, or a "sinking feeling," is often discomforting. So we must confront our feelings toward this psychic and present change in the way we hold our energy. Once we accept this real change and allow it to be, sinking is possible.

In one sense we sink our weight; in another, we sink our energy (lowering our attention and surrendering our upper positioning); but both processes work simultaneously. We must concentrate on our feet and the feeling in the feet as they constantly relate and readjust relationship to the earth. This relaxing or sinking into the earth provides our source of movement. It is this tendency to fall or be pulled to the earth that allows the force of our movements to occur. It is the transference of weight from one foot to the other that allows us most of our actions and power. This transference is a relaxing or releasing of one leg to favor the other.

Adjust the waist and legs to accommodate a force.

It is the intrinsic strength, or the elastic binding quality inherent in the tissues of the body, that supports the weighted leg, and the intrinsic energy (feeling) that fills the leg that is doing the supporting. This shifting of weight by relaxing is the way we use the earth's force to move our own bodies. The center and our attention on it accepts the force generated from this action to direct the body in some specific fashion. Therefore, it is imperative that we keep our attention on the feet, legs and pelvis, and use the force of gravity to source and manipulate our movement.

Support from below.

Being aligned with all that is grounding is extremely important in any physical activity. The principle of grounding is also
applicable to mental and emotional activity, psychic activity, and
any other activity where an objective relationship is occurring.
However, the form and appearance of the grounding will take on
radically different dimensions. We must begin to consider what
grounding really is. Certainly it appears to have something to do
with the earth and with gravity. But what is gravity? What, for that
matter, is the earth? When we begin to look into the great forces
that are involved, the principles that appear in attraction, relativi-
ty, union, or unifying force, as well as expansion and radiance,
we start to see that gravity is not just a mere "fact of the planet."
It is a profound force and possibility. It is representative of a prime
principle that founds the being of an entity. Consider this deeply.

5. BEING WHOLE AND TOTAL (Unity)

Integrity is an essential aspect of this "Five-Word" Principle. Our
first consideration in this matter is that of the unification of the
whole body. The whole body must not only work together, but
the limbs must be subservient to the dictates of the whole, specifically to the center. In addition to using the word "unify," I like the
phrase "being whole and total." Once again, this is inclusive of
all that we call unity; it simply expands into the associations these
words elicit which are true of this principle. "Whole" and "total"
give us a sense of being complete, full, with no holes in or around
our body or integrity, and with *all* of our composition present and
involved.

Ending the letter:

> Use your whole body in unison and as one piece, centered
> in the pelvis, with the most important priority given to the
> center and legs. All of the body, although relaxed, should act
> as one piece. The only way to do this successfully in a real
> sense, and also keep the body relaxed, is to unify the energy
> and being and let the body follow the energy's unity.

It is important that these priorities are met: (1) the lower over
the upper, (2) the center over extremities, (3) the inside over the
outside, (4) the earth over the body, and (5) the feet, center and

legs over the chest, shoulders, and arms. When I say 'over' I mean that they actually move the other part, and take precedence. All of the main joints must combine and be in harmony with one another; e.g., if the hips move, the shoulders follow—same time, same direction. It is also necessary to 'look' in the direction of the waist's movement or principle activity, to help direct the body as one piece.

Every action should have its source in the feet, and its direction from the center. It is not enough just to move the arms at the same time as the hips—the arms must be moved *by* the hips! This point is often neglected. In my discussion of "sinking," I mentioned that the upper body must rest on the lower. If this is done, and the upper body is directed to do nothing but relax, then it will be moved by the center and legs entirely, and the upper and lower will act as one piece. But you must "feel" this and make it so; otherwise, it will not happen.

This unification can be a delicate process. If muscles are exerted here and there, or held in place, then real unity is not possible. These acts will break up the unity of the body because they act independently. The body parts must not only move together in the same direction, but must also move for the same purpose.

This point is often not grasped fully. If we have a movement directed for one purpose, the whole body must relax and be directed by the center and feet. If muscles are exerted to push out "these" parts and contract "those," then others must be used to check the first and hold the second in order to maintain balance, and this increases tension (which only increases the "sensation" of strength, and this is not the same as the accomplishment of strength). As a result, we have many areas that are "dead," held in place through tension, and others that are terribly restricted because muscles are serving antagonistic roles toward one another. We even find in this case, which is by far the most common one, that some parts are moving in the wrong direction to accomplish the purpose at hand. This state is known as "fighting yourself"!

To resolve this dilemma, we must relax the myriad of muscles that could and would act inappropriately, so that the entire weight, energy and attention all work together in one movement which springs solely from the feet. It is a delicate process, but by relaxing, allowing the major joints to move together, and following the priorities mentioned earlier, we can encourage this process.

Fill out and be complete, yet be empty and with nothing to protect.

As I said, the only way to make the entire relaxed body function in such a way is to give up the body and follow the "feeling-awareness." Then we have only to unify this feeling. If we form a union with our whole mind activity and our entire sense of being, then the energy will unify. Keeping the body relaxed, we may direct this feeling-sense for any purpose and the body must follow.

Integrity, like "relaxing," "grounding," "being calm," and "centering" permeates all aspects of our activity. Our whole body must unify (one body), our energy must unify (one feeling), and our mind must unify (one mind). We must go further and achieve the very important unification of mind, energy, and body, to form one being. This harmony and union of mind, energy, and body is essential to Cheng Hsin. However, we must not think of it as something too difficult or too easy to accomplish, but must do what we can now, and when that's accomplished, continue.

Taken even further, union must occur not only with our being, but with other beings and the earth as well. Later in the book, I will deal specifically with the union of relationship that occurs in interaction with another. This principle of union, being whole and total, or integrity, warrents investigation far beyond the body-being considerations we are dealing with here. This entire book could be said to deal with the Integrity of Being as a multi-dimensional and many-faceted event, and at the same time as a simple and singular one.

Concluding Chapter One

The Five Cheng Hsin Principles of Body-Being:

        1. Being calm—being present
        2. Relaxing
        3. Centering
        4. Grounding
        5. Being whole and total

These few essentials reach the greatest depths and allow for the highest development. Do not take them lightly; seek to accomplish them completely and in all activity, and to discover the actual Principle that brings them into being.

Direct the energy (feeling-attention) with a calm presence of Being. Relax the body so that it is mobile and allows the energy and feeling to sink and circulate and follow this direction. Let the body act as a unit, moving from the center. Be in harmony and alignment with this "integrity of being."

> *The problem with formed teaching lies in the difficulty of maintaining the transmission of the root-condition (not-knowing) while the appearance of form (knowing) keeps them busy; without losing the only real development while 'forming' is going on.*

Since Cheng Hsin is difficult to comprehend fully and use immediately, I have broken its study down into the fundamental principles that appear to arise from "listening" to Cheng Hsin. From hearing and studying these principles and design, you can begin to intuit for yourself what Cheng Hsin is, and from the unthought experience of Cheng Hsin create what is appropriate.

Chapter Two

A Look at Body-Being Development

Eight Points on Structuring the Body-Being

The alignment of the body to its functional design is very important to realizing an effortless power in its use. To further this alignment, I offer these points on posture, structure, and orientation. These points are again part of one whole. They are representative of the basic qualities and considerations that determine our posture and so our movements.

I want to draw attention to the danger that often arises when people slip into thinking that these points are to be practiced and remembered only when standing still, or in formal postures or sets. This is *definitely not* the case. They should be followed continuously, at every moment and in every stage of activity, as well as in ritual technique and functional interaction. After all, movement *is* only changing posture.

At this point we must consider: what is the body's functional design? This investigation must enter every movement and functional activity. Only then can we endeavor to align with what is found to be most effortlessly powerful.

It is in so doing that we get our first real sense of changeless changing in which from beginning to end we have done nothing but this one thing. These Eight Points and Five Principle considerations are our immediate and sole endeavor, so that through all of our twisting, turning, shifting, stepping here and there, we have indeed done only one thing! Yet we have apparently changed and changed again. It is here that we begin to experience the joy of this work. Through constant adherence to this principle we begin to see what is continuously and completely unchanged, and to develop insight into the very nature of activity. Over time, the source of the activity emerges and thus becomes apparent to us.

A tuning fork will not make a sound unless it is hit. The physical manifestation of the tuning fork is not enough; there must be the act of hitting, and its vibration, to permit its function. So we must realize that action, and especially creative activity (the act of hitting the fork), must work within the design of the instrument or functioning body to direct the energy (fork vibration) towards the purpose at hand. When these work together, we will feel much more whole, complete, and competent.

The Eight Points

1. ALIGN WITH GRAVITY

If you held a string in one hand and attached a weight to the other end and let it go, which way would it fall? If you threw a stone into a lake, where would it go? Heavier things naturally fall to a lower position. The air, water, and earth all have a definite order to them, the heavier always settling below the lighter. As I noted in the discussion of grounding, the direction of our weight and energy is downward and we must align to this orientation. In correspondence with our vertical relationship to the earth, we must allow the structure of our body to align with the force that is constantly present to it.

If we relax our tissues, we are free to align the body in any way we wish. If we lean or cave in or out, we must hold these parts tense to keep the body from falling. But if we "stack" all of the body parts so that they fall naturally in accord with gravity, we need only use the minimum amount of energy to hold up the body. This is especially critical in movement, since any discrepancies in our posture when standing are magnified by momentum and the constant need to change yet maintain balance.

Essentially we must balance the body so that each part below directly supports the parts above. Everything not in immediate functional use hangs down; that which is in use should also drain downward, and be held up with minimal effort. Thus, this point corresponds to the principles of sinking and relaxing. Because of the necessary interdependency the parts have to one another, attention to this point will also help unify the body. So even as you move, feel as if you could support a book on your head, keeping the spine straight and vertical. This increases awareness of the body's relationship to gravity.

Even though our body is balanced, when I say let it go completely, why don't we fall down? We do fall down. But because we are balanced we can direct the falling into the feet. If we are balanced then our feet are under us, and our legs, pelvis, spine, etc. fall one into the other; where else could they go? If we stack dishes on top of each other, the top dishes aren't going to fall to the floor unless we unbalance the stack. You see, we are already "on the floor"; our feet have fallen as far as they can. What must occur is an alignment of every body part so that the net result of the "fall" of them is a vertical descent at the bottom of the feet. We must align with the force or "pull" that appears in falling. We must align with what is called gravity.

2. THE KNEE, HEEL, AND TOE
This is basically the continuation of Point One. I use these points about the knee because attention to them is the easiest way to correct a majority of errors in alignment. If the center of your body sinks, or presses, into the center of your foot, you actually feel more of the weight and pressure on the heel-center part of the foot, since the leg attaches to the ankle which is nearer the rear of the foot. Therefore, the movement of the knee should be directed down the leg and into the heel. The knee should not move in any direction that will not end up pressing the heel. If this important point is properly done, you need not worry about your front knee passing over your toe; it cannot.

Furthermore, the front of the knee points or bends in the same or parallel direction as the toe. So if the toe turns in or out, the knee makes the same turn. This allows the design of the knee, which is a hinge joint, to operate as it should. To twist the knee sideways, which is in any direction other than the direction of the toe, puts a lot of torque and strain on the knee. It is then being used badly and cannot support the body weight easily. In this way much of the power that could be used by aligning with the design is lost. Therefore, the knee should move towards or press into the heel, and point in the direction of the toe.

Proper support increases the amount of intrinsic strength that you can use from your direct connection with the earth. It also prevents the weight from actually missing your feet or otherwise being misplaced, thus straining your ankles and taxing your knees.

Very important to this structuring is the positioning of the pelvis. The pelvis and hips should remain between the two feet. The sacrum should not stick out to the rear, but should take a vertical position along with the lower vertebrae. Just as the front knee does not push forward of the ankle, the pelvis or hip does not pass behind the back foot, nor to the right or left of the line between the feet. Keeping the pelvis between the feet simply assists the weight of the body to fall towards the feet, and not elsewhere. In this way we can directly support the spine and the whole body. Supported directly, the body can then press the foot properly with no breaks or contortions. Establishing these two points, you will feel yourself much more directly in contact with the earth.

3. SHIFTING THE WEIGHT

Because our principle power is intrinsic and therefore compressive in nature, how we shift our weight from one leg to the other is very important. Adhering to the principle goal of effortless power, we relax one leg towards the other; we never brace up or move towards both at the same time. Therefore, the tendency is for one leg to carry more weight than the other. Remember to release and relax the leg that does not carry most of the weight. This allows more freedom to move and less dependency on any one place where we might stand. With one foot free, we can immediately adjust our steps or waist and legs without preliminary movement. If the weight were in both legs, we would first have to shift it to one or other before acting, and run the risk of being caught in rigidity or in loss of balance ("double-weighted"), unable to move properly. Freezing the joints (being rigid) and losing balance limit our ability to draw on the earth and our intrinsic strength.

All of this allows us to shift the weight as if dropping it into the ground. In this way, we compress or squeeze our body into— and as a result, as if "up from"—the ground. Letting go of the leg that presently carries most of the body weight begins a drop or fall slightly toward the ground as the weight shifts toward the other foot. In this way, as the weight arrives on the other foot, it is then squeezed or compressed in this foot—as if we are going to stand up yet fall down at the same time. It is important to shift the weight like this in order to stay in alignment with gravity and in contact with the ground, and so "come from" (get power from the compression into) the ground. Shifting the weight is one of the fundamental ways to translate compressive power into a horizontal movement. The other method is the use of a spiraling movement out of one foot.

The Center Presses the Earth

If the center and the whole body are to move around in space, they need to relate to the earth and to the gravitational pull of the body mass in relationship to the earth, for motivation. This is where pressing the foot comes in.

The center (and the feeling-attention abiding there) should move vertically in relationship to the foot. Horizontal movement is only possible with a vertical relationship, straight up and down, between our mass and the earth. To align with this most effectively, we press our center straight downward into the weighted foot, increasing the pressure of the foot against the earth. This pressure in turn gives us the necessary motivating force to propel the center in any manner that we wish. Without this pressure the center would not move at all—if it were floating in space it could not move. So we must remember: if we want to move horizontally we must never neglect the vertical movement. We are continuously establishing a pressure by having the center sink into the foot that we're standing on, again and again, with every movement we make from foot to foot, or on the same foot.

Thus, pressing the center into the foot creates power in our movements, allowing us to propel the center according to our dictates. It is the "plug," the source of energy for the center, but not the intelligence. The intelligence abides in the center so that movement gets its direction from there, but the movement gets its power through the foot and from the earth. Therefore, our attention must lie (as far as energy, movement, strength and power are concerned) in the center, the foot, and the earth.

Although the legs remain quite relaxed, when the center presses on one of them, it becomes taut like a stretched elastic band. This "stretching" or compression of the leg, and an increase of pressure in the foot, is one of the main components of intrinsic strength. The foot should be considered as if penetrating the earth and the pressure as moving up and down at the same time, as if we are pushing the earth away from us rather than pushing ourselves away from the earth.

As the breath presses into the center region itself, simultaneously move the feeling-energy down into the foot and press the earth. This whole movement initiates the use of intrinsic strength. The use of intrinsic strength comes and goes (like the breath comes in and goes out), since it acts as an expression of power, not as a constant flow of energy. However, a great deal of intrinsic power can be maintained throughout as a current or constant activity. By pressing, sinking, relaxing and dropping the feeling-attention down, we create an incredible amount of energy and pressure through the legs, which is instantaneously available to us. I will talk more about intrinsic force in later parts of this book.

Pressing the foot can be done very quickly. Whether we are moving fast or standing still, the same thing occurs. We can move deliberately onto one foot, bringing a lot of power to bear, or we can dance quickly from foot to foot, and still bring the power to bear. In either case, it is the center pressing the foot, that is all. We do not need a great deal of time to do this; it can be done in a moment. We can suddenly press into the foot and motivate the center quickly, or we can do it over a longer period of time with a very deliberate "drawing-of-the-bow" type movement such as we would find in shifting the weight.

Be sure to keep your feet under you. When moving around it is well advised to be sure-footed and have a very even, continuously reestablished pressing of the foot with the center, so that you never lose equilibrium, balance, power or the source of your movement. Therefore, it is ill-advised to be caught in rigidity, or pressing both feet, because then there is a moment when the motivation of the center is split and confused. Maintain connection to the ground through pressure in the feet; otherwise, the center will float, lacking its ground and power for movement, and therefore cannot move appropriately, quickly or suddenly.

Like every other point, the center pressing the foot is practiced in all movement. Adherence to the water-drop energy* helps establish this point as a matter of course.

---

*See Chapter Four, pages 56 to 59.

The Breath

When we breathe, we wish to sink that breath into the lower abdomen, leaving the chest relaxed. Let's look briefly at how this is done. The first thing to do is relax the internal organs. We will find the more gas and less exercise these have, the harder this is to do. In any case, this particular form of breathing is excellent for aiding the digestion and exercising these organs.

Concentrate the breath down at the very bottom of the pelvic girdle; fill from down there first, then expand it into the lower abdomen below the navel. This creates a pressure in the area within the pelvis, sacrum, lower vertebrae and abdominal wall. This pressure may act like a pressure cooker and increase the connection between the upper and lower body; it also assists in the coordination and directing of force. The breath may be done here when inhaling by compressing the tissues downward and so drawing air into the lungs, or air may be "stored up," then the lungs partially emptied and the rest of the breath pressed down. Either way, the chest and upper body relax and collapse; they do not force closure, or push down. As the upper body relaxes, its weight gently falls down and presses the breath to the lower parts. Thus it springs back naturally. This helps give tenacity to the trunk and soften the upper function.

As the breath is lowered into the abdomen, the intrinsic energy that follows this movement must immediately be pressed into the feet. Most importantly, do not force it, and do not be too preoccupied with the breath. It is better to concentrate on the principles and points than to be overly concerned with the breathing. If the breath does not fall easily, don't worry; with this kind of breathing the organs will relax, and then the breath will fall naturally.

4. UNLOCKING THE BODY

All of the joints of the body and all body parts must be relaxed and free. A joint only functions as a joint if it is allowed to be free moving, open, and unlocked. Put attention on allowing the joints to bend and rotate with ease, as if well oiled. Release your hold on all parts of the body so that they can align themselves to the design of things and fulfill their function. The following are some of the major areas to check and unlock.

Fall into the legs and feet

This is a specific check on the legs and feet. Relaxing them appears externally, but must be done internally. The feet, when pressed, should feel as if they "squish" into the ground—like a suction cup pushed down spreads on the surface that it's on. The feet must be relaxed so they spread naturally, and so that you can feel the ground with them. You should also be able to discern minor changes in the weight that rests on them, and how these changes affect the whole body. If a lopsided shift is about to occur, you should feel it in your feet, and instantly change the footing or the shift. It is not enough just to stand up; you want to stand relaxed, balanced, and directly into your whole foot. Don't think that relaxing does not apply to the foot; it must be supple also. The ankle must relax and be free-floating, so that the foot won't be pulled off as a result of the inability of the ankle to relax and handle shifts in weight that occur.

Relaxing the legs may seem contrary to standing up, and you should relax them almost to this point. When the legs (and pelvis) relax properly, the knee will tend to point in the same direction as the toe, no matter which way you point the toe. Do not hold the hip joint where the leg attaches to the pelvis. This common tendency results in the legs not falling naturally. Relax.

As we discussed in Point Three, one leg is continuously relaxing and emptying. Unless you are constantly relaxing, this will not occur properly. The leg that is full must be regarded like a relaxed rubber band: if pulled (or pressed in this case) it becomes more taut, but the rubber band itself never "tenses up" or contracts! So it is with your leg. No matter how "compressed" it becomes, it still must remain relaxed, and this must be a conscious and deliberate process.

Open the pelvis

The entire pelvic structure should be loosened. The pelvis is an area most people keep tight and immobile. Because of its nature and usual lack of use, it is easy to overlook. The muscles are large in and around it, and difficult to loosen unless you "get in touch" with them. Because most people don't know they hold their pelvis, it is hard for them to relax it. When the pelvis massively relaxes for the first time, it is astounding. The whole area seems literally to drop, and you suddenly feel more grounded and in your feet. From an old martial classic:

"The pelvis should be as if boneless."

Restriction in the pelvis is the cause of many disabilities; holding the pelvis improperly or tightly causes severe problems and severance in many other areas of the body. The way you hold yourself, for example, is affected directly by the state of the pelvis. The inability of the knee to point with the toe is most often the result of a tight hip joint. The feet turning outward, or riding on one part instead of evenly, is frequently solved by relaxing the pelvis. And as mentioned, we must always take care that the pelvis remains between the two feet; otherwise bodily integrity and structural alignment and balance will be in jeopardy. Also relax and let settle all the internal organs that rest in and over the pelvic area, as well as the muscles around them.

Relax the upper body

The shoulder joints and surrounding area should be allowed to drop to a natural position and should be made very loose and free. You must watch so as not to use the shoulder itself to perform actions that can easily be done with the center and legs. The chest should depress and be empty of strength, although the back should remain straight. As you relax the chest, fill the belly. Always keep the abdomen relaxed, and let the belly hang loose. Unless functional design demands otherwise, when the hands are up the elbows should point downward. In general, the elbows are dropped along with everything else, or positioned in such a way that gives the most effortless effectiveness, which frequently means pointing in a line from elbow to hand in the direction of force. The head balances on the spine, and the hands are only barely lifted. Essentially, the upper body gives up its function to the lower. It may feel exasperatingly useless, but if this is the case, you know you are making progress!

Be freely balanced

We must always maintain balance, and more than this, our balance should not be dependent on or be influenced by any occurring forces. In other words, the force or momentum of our own movement should not put our balance in jeopardy, nor should the force or movement of another. We must remain constantly balanced and our balance must not be dependent on anything transient.

To be freely balanced means that our balance is not influenced in the slightest by external forces, neither another applying force to us or we to them. The only way to do this is to understand and use intrinsic strength. Any resistance or exertion will always either throw us off balance or lock our balance into dependency on the forces or masses at hand.

Most people rarely experience balance when standing, but actually maintain a constant state of imbalance. Simply because you don't fall down doesn't mean you're balanced; try not moving any muscle when you stand and see how long it takes to fall down. You make constant, and usually unconscious, correction to manage your loss of balance. When something is balanced it is at rest; it needs no managing. So you are invited to make a distinction between managing off-balance and being balanced. You may not always be balanced, but you should know the difference.

We must always endeavor to be freely balanced, which is empowered by being relaxed and opening the joints, so that our body may be at rest even in motion. We must always "stand on our own feet" and never lean on or depend on someone else to maintain our balance. This is a profound point and requires a great deal of consideration. It is very subtle and yet can make a great difference in our abilities if fully understood.

5. INTEGRATE, UNIFY AND COORDINATE ALL BODY PARTS

The differentiation of the human body into specialized parts permits movement and the adoption of a variety of shapes. When the connecting points of these sections (joints) are held tightly, we lose the capacity to change and move freely. Yet when they are in disharmony and discord, when they are motivated into action that is independent or segmented, we lose power, balance, coordination, and more. So, without tightening up or binding the joints, we need to bring into harmony and unity every single part of the body.

Lok Hap (Six Coordinations)

One consideration in movement is the unification and coordination of the three major sections of the body: legs, arms, and trunk. Through these we derive the *lok hap. Lok hap* deals specifically with the unity of the Body-Being. It focuses on the six major joints and other aspects of unity and function.

The first three aspects of *lok hap* are bodily functions. The coordination of the six major joints:

1. Hips and shoulders move together
2. Knees and elbows move together
3. Feet and hands move together

This means that these parts actually move together, coordinating with and matching each other. The lower and center parts take priority over and initiate movement in the upper and outer parts. If a foot goes forward, it is always coordinated with and in relationship to the hand, and both are directed by the center. The hip turns with the shoulder, and being in between, the elbows and knees must move together also. This totally unifies the whole body. Be careful to do this with devotion and it will produce great changes in your ability. Turning or twisting parts also correspond, but remember, the center moves all.

A progression for the training and development of the *lok hap*:

a. Concentrate on moving the hips and shoulders together, along with the spine and head, to create all actions.

b. Then have the hips move the elbows.

c. Let the knee's pressure in the heel move the hips and elbows, and keep the knee pointing with the toe.

d. Concentrate on the action of the center and pelvis, moving together and in cooperation with the feet. All actions then come from the pressing of the feet and direction of the center and hips.

e. Finally, connect the hands with the actions of the hips and feet, so that they *do not move* unless the center (or hips) move them! The hands, pelvis and feet then are in unison, and act as one.

Study and become adept at one point before moving to the next. When you accomplish all five, your *lok hap* will be functional.

The second three aspects of lok hap are dimensional functions:

4. Being *(Hsin)* and mind together
5. Mind and life force together
6. Life force and action, or power, together

The Being and mind unify to create a real intelligence, and this calm direction moves the feeling-attention. The three centers —the head (between the brows), the heart (center of the chest), and the body's center *(tan t'ien)*—all work together physically as well as internally. The feeling-attention is directed by *Hsin*, and works to direct all actions and any power that is created. This power manifests physically and springs from the tissues and their intrinsic quality, but is created internally and is a function of calm direction.

Trust in the Being's dictates, not the body's strength.

Nose with navel

The movement of the head plays an important part in the direction of the body's movements. It can either increase proper bodily function or restrict it altogether. If your head is held in place, your body will not move freely. To unify the body in action, it is very helpful for the movement of the head to direct or correspond to the whole body's desired action. If you wish to turn left, for example, you should turn your head left at the same time as your body. To point the nose in the same direction that the navel points is a helpful way to increase this ability.

In the beginning, you should put attention on keeping the nose and navel pointing together. This will increase unity and make whole-body movements much easier. If, for example, you want to turn and face the opposite direction, you can essentially just "look" suddenly to the rear, keeping nose and navel moving together. This turns the pelvis at the same time as the head. You can now turn your whole body around more efficiently and quickly, in one movement and as one piece. This is so because you turn from the pelvis to create the act, but it is directed by turning the head. Eventually, as you become more advanced and this point is adhered to, you may begin to understand this as the "mind's eye" directing the purpose of a unified body. With experience, it may be done without detriment, even though the nose is not exactly on a line with the navel. But this should not be attempted until the nose and navel can work together securely, and the purpose for such an exercise is fully understood. In brief, this point is a general unification of the body, specifically top and bottom, but also encourages all of the major joints to work in unison.

Unifying the Three Essentials

I enjoy Cheng's way of representing the Three Essentials (man, heaven, earth) as life-force cultivation (for our present purpose they are conditions achieved in the Body-Being):

I. Man: The Ch'i Circulates
   a. Ch'i goes from shoulders to fingers
   b. Ch'i goes from thigh to sole of the foot
   c. Ch'i goes from sacrum to top of the head
II. Earth: The Ch'i Penetrates the Bones
   a. Ch'i goes to the Center Region (Tan T'ien)
   b. Ch'i focuses on the sole
   c. Ch'i permeates the entire body.
III. Heaven: Interpreting the Energy
   a. "Hear" the energy (Listening)
   b. Understand the energy (Receiving)
   c. Transcend energy

The first may be achieved by relaxing, draining tension and opening the body to let the energy and feeling-attention flow naturally; the second, by sinking, concentrating the ch'i down, and "feeling" (thus unifying) the entire body. The ch'i will then expand or radiate throughout. The third essential is realized through contemplation and experience. It is sometimes useful to think of the three essentials as simply mind, energy, and body. But first we must use our mind to free and "make natural" our body, by following the Eight Posture Points and Five Principles.

Integrate the body

The pelvis (and sacrum) must be directly under your upper body, and directly over the feet, so that it is centered between the lower and upper. Then it should fall naturally. As you move, maintain this state and remember that your pelvis (and everything else) must *continuously* be falling into a natural position. Don't worry about placing the feet at any particular distance; let them fall naturally and comfortably. Even a very short step is correct if the principles are followed.

Start out slowly at first, adhering *strictly* to the points as you move. Start with a check on the Eight Points while still, then begin to move. If you move *one inch* without doing all points, stop and go back until you can do it. Practice all your actions and sets this way. Remember, not one inch without paying attention to every minute detail! Eventually, you will be able to move much faster. By adhering to these points you will find that your actions do not feel the same as before; they are more efficient and achieve their purpose with no exertion or strain. They become simple. Concentrate on the whole body, not just the arms. The arms must just "go along for the ride."

6. FUNCTIONAL PRIORITIES

In a truly functional body, the upper is subservient to the lower, and the inner directs the outer. Therefore, the closer to the source of the body's center, the planet's center, and the source of the creating itself, the higher the priority. The earth takes precedence (priority) over the body. The feet and legs move (take precedence over) and give motivation to the center, and the center directs the purpose of the whole body. The upper parts of the body are moved by the lower parts of the body. If the hips move, then the shoulders move; the feet move and then the hands move. The inner parts take precedence over the outer parts (the elbows take precedence over the hands, and so on).

This is why in the water-drop energy*, the greatest mass lies below the center region and beneath the ground, as well as being positioned in the middle or vertical center line of the body. The shape of the water-drop itself represents that priority situation, as you can observe by noticing that the mass is below, while above narrows and comes to a point. It must be remembered that the shape is spherical (three-dimensional) and not merely planar.

We must also refer to the priority given to those things unseen: Nothing *(wu chi)*, or the source of Being, is given priority over anything appearing. Being takes precedence over the activity that is mind, so emptiness and openness are held requisite for any thought or feeling to occur. In other words, *Hsin*, or the source, origin and union of conceptualization, feeling and awareness, takes precedence, is prior to and leads these activities as well as the energy of the body. The energy of the body—feeling-attention in the form of bodily impulse—moves and takes precedence over the

---

*See Chapter Four, pages 56 to 59.

physical movement of the body. The whole domain of life force, which includes all activities that arise out of Being, again goes from what we consider "inner" to "outer," from insubstantial, essentially radiant, empty and formless to solid, objective and substantial.

Remember that reference and adherence to the proper priorities are constant and continuous. When we experience the "rationality" behind the functional relationship the distinctions of our body-being have to one another, then we will comprehend the necessity to integrate and prioritize, or assign functional roles. The difficulty lies not only in establishing it but in maintaining it, especially in situations where tendency pulls us into reactive habits that distort the priorities I have just mentioned.

7. CREATING THE OPENING FOR INTRINSIC STRENGTH

Making the connections and alignments in the body which allow its intrinsic strength to be used naturally and easily could be a complex affair. However, we can create an opening for the intrinsic strength to function, by falling into certain states of being, or producing body-being "feeling" orientations. We fall into the alignment that is necessary for effective action without having to think it through (something we would really be hard-pressed to do anyway). We set up the proper relationship of body parts to one another, and empower the proper timing in their use. All these things are accomplished within a principle that ultimately manifests as effortless power. The following body-being orientation is a large step towards discovering that principle.

Whenever a part of the body lifts up we must concentrate on what I call "marrow draining." This is basically feeling as if the strength, weight, and very "marrow" of that part, drain into the lower mass.

> *The body can act subject to change and external influence only if it has no 'mind of its own.'*

"Rag-doll syndrome"

Prior to getting in touch with this "draining energy," you should first experience the "rag-doll syndrome": relaxing the tissues totally, loosening all of the joints and completely letting the body go so that it obtains a state like a rag-doll—completely floppy, loose and limp. It is advisable to spend a considerable amount of time developing this alone. Working from the center, throw your body around without any impulse or motivation whatsoever to any of the limbs or parts. The limbs fly or are tossed around *only* as the center moves them. For example, if you were to throw an arm via spinning the center quickly so that the arm were projected outward, it would only go as far as the motivation of the center has allowed and then would just fall wherever it fell.

With practice you will learn how to project the limbs, parts, and segments of the body, completely relaxed and without impulse, in whatever direction you want, solely by directing your center to propel them there. Moving the legs in this fashion is often a more difficult task. Each leg must also be like a piece of "dead meat," moving only in whatever direction the pelvis throws it. An absolute minimum amount of force is used to stand. You will thus develop an accurate sense of exactly how to move any part of the body solely from the center. This study/practice takes center movement out of the realm of the vague and mysterious, and makes it real.

You must remember that not only should the limbs be relaxed and loose, but that you should also move that relaxation and looseness into the chest, spine, abdomen and the pelvis, making those flaccid also. Obviously, because of their bulk these do not flop around as easily, but you should feel them and literally flop them around with the rest of the body. Once the whole body, including the internal organs and the bones and all of the muscles, are totally relaxed, you will have attained a different state of being, and a very energizing and nourishing one. From this state the "hand up—you down" principle can be applied.

"Hand up—you down"

Once we relax the arm, chest, and upper body and subject them to the dictates of the lower body, while sinking the feeling-attention down into the earth and concentrating attention on the center, we begin to get a sense of "hand up—you down." The "you" in "hand up—you down" refers to the feeling-awareness that we experience as "a" or "the" primary aspect of being or being a self; it is the "force" of being. When a limb is lifted (this includes the foot or any other part of the body, but is figuratively referred to as the hand), we feel a sensation of draining away from the hand, arm, shoulder, and chest area as the hand moves up; as if we were actually draining into the legs, feet, and floor, and as if the body were falling away from the limb that is being used. This sensation appears to be in contradiction to moving energy into the limb that is functioning; however, paradoxical as it may sound, the inverse is actually true, for we achieve a much greater degree of power when the proper priorities are established.

When doing any movement, lifting any hand or limb, the "hand up—you down" principle should be applied. As the hand goes out to hit someone, for example, or just raises up, the energy drains from the arm, as sand drains through an hourglass, but more quickly. As the hand touches the opponent the strength drains out of the arm and is concentrated down into the feet and legs. Power is achieved simply by lifting the hand and aligning the body to the immediate purpose. A great deal more power is achieved in this way because the energy comes from the earth, legs, and the intrinsic nature of the body, and not from the strength in the arm. The arm remains much more relaxed and capable of a superior kind of movement, of which a tense or strong arm is completely incapable. In adopting this principle we find that our abilities are increased manyfold: borrowing, following, changing, speed, and great duration in the period of time that the arm can be used, employing a minimum amount of force with a maximum amount of power.

By relaxing the tissues, ("rag-doll syndrome") and internal-izing this "hand up—you down" principle, we can achieve a dra-matic elongation of body and limbs (in excess of the normal distance within which we usually think that a blow must take place). This extended reach can occur because the joints open and the tissues loosen so that with the direction of the extending or outreaching energy, a blow can be placed at a much greater distance than the opponent is expecting.

The "hand up—you down" point is probably akin to the expe-rience that Cheng Man Ch'ing describes as the disappearance of his shoulders. He felt at one point as if he had no shoulders, his limbs were acting directly from the center, and his strength came directly from the foot. Instantly, he became more powerful and could not be defeated. With "hand up—you down," the disappear-ance of strength, or what we consider strength, in the upper part of the body is necessary so that a new kind of power may be generated. This power is not created so much from our muscular strength as it is from maintaining the proper priorities, and a movement or flow of energy that we normally do not associate with strength.

The method itself is somewhat like hanging onto a branch of a tree, and then relaxing away from the branch so that our weight is falling down and our body is as relaxed as possible. In addition, we drop the sense of being, the sense of strength, and the sense of control out of the limb that is being raised. It is the same when a foot goes up; we drain away from the foot that is going up, and into the foot that is on the ground.

This point creates the opening necessary for the use of intrinsic strength.

8. EIGHT ATTITUDE AWARENESS—BEING THREE-DIMENSIONAL

To realize this distinction in feeling-awareness (or "energy"), we must first situate our attention in the center of the body. From there, we can radiate quite freely and equally, in all directions. In the past, this concept has been interpreted as the four sides and four corners surrounding the body. I have expanded this distinction to include an awareness of and absolute inclusion of three-dimensional reality.

The eight attitudes are, briefly:

1. Front	2. Rear
3. Left	4. Right
5. Up	6. Down
7. Inside	8. Outside

In a basic spatial sense, the eight attitudes are all-encompassing. The front includes all which is to the front of you, as the rear includes everything behind you. However, they refer not only to the space that extends from your body outward in those directions, but also to that aspect of your body itself. The rear is the back of the body, such as the spine; the front is the chest, face, and the direction of most of the perceptive organs. The left and right sides also include the sides of the body and the space of those directions, and all include the sensitivity of the energy or "aura" that occupies that position.

Furthermore, we must be aware of the relationship of each

aspect with the others. Not only does "up" include the top of the head and above, or "down" the bottom of the feet and below, but also the interaction and interplay of what up and down are, and how they must co-exist to create one another, and coordinate to enhance one another. "When attacking with the front, do not forget the rear" is a statement to that effect.

"Inside" refers to the internal organs, bones and to their spatial relationship, and "outside," to the external muscles and skin, as well as to the space outside of the body. It also refers to the relationship of that which is not physical, tangible, or formed in any way with that which is. The "mind," awareness, energy, aura, and sensitivities may be considered inside (internal), and the body outside (external). Although energy and feeling-attention are formless in the sense that they have no particular or definite objective boundaries, they occur in relationship to physical conditions, and therefore have a nature, the form of which is determined freely by the direction of Being, and may appear to be the link between absolute formlessness *(Hsin)* and the physical or objective condition. The third interpretation is of that which exists (formed or formlessly) and that which does not exist (Absolute Nothing—*wu chi*).

In adopting this Eight Attitude Awareness, we should first empty the mind and center the attention; second, open all the joints and adopt a posture in alignment with the above seven points; and third, expand the awareness to include all of these eight aspects of the body-being. Then there is no hole left unfilled!

Open the field of awareness (feeling-attention).

At this time I wish to remind you that you must work with what you have now. Attainment of anything comes essentially in degrees (although sudden breakthroughs occasionally occur). Mastery of something on a mundane level is necessary for a continued progress toward mastery on other levels. Even among "masters" there are degrees of attainment. I want you to be the heart of your own accomplishment. Through discovering, giving being to, and following these five principles and eight points you are free to understand the core of the Cheng Hsin Body-Being; and by learning them well, you will make rapid and profound progress that will exceed your most optimistic goals.

Some posture points to remember

I would like to list a few points on structure that are helpful to remember while you practice. This list is not necessarily complete, but too many points would not be useful. Here are twelve:

1. Keep the feet flat; instep down, foot relaxed and solid (firmly rooted).

2. Relax the body and "drain" it into the feet.

3. Center action directs the whole body.

4. Hips move the elbows.

5. The nose points with the navel or energy; the knees point with the toes; the elbows point into the functional target.

6. Stay calm, sunk (drop the energy below the earth with your feeling-awareness), forming a root deep wherever you stand and press the knee toward the heel.

7. Move with smooth and unified action, with no independent or segmented movement.

8. Use intrinsic strength—relax the tissues and align the body so that power is achieved through movement alone, not tension.

9. Maintain agility with the pelvis, legs, and feet. Use "rubber legs" with the weight of the upper body resting on them; "keep the feet under you," and always be freely balanced.

10. Keep the back straight, tail in, and align with gravity.

11. Breathe continuously and freely into the center region by relaxing and sinking.

12. Use Being to will the actions of the body through feeling-impulse, or the "force of being." The body will follow, and much faster and more effectively than if you concentrate only on the body movement, strength, or result.

Chapter Three

Establishing a Relationship With Cheng Hsin

Questioning our own event

There are many ways to approach internal martial arts, and some are real and functional approaches. But in my opinion the only true approach throughout should be one of insight and understanding. In trying to deepen our understanding, remember that depth of vision comes from two points of view, namely our two eyes; each views the world slightly differently, which adds quality and depth to the view. If this is so for our seeing, it certainly must be so for our learning and relating. One point of view, our own, is not enough; relationship can only be had by more than one. Learning, insight, understanding and ability all exist as a function of relationship. Realizing beyond our own point of view is necessary for a deeper understanding.

"Hsing I" translates as something like the "appearance" or "form" of Consciousness. From this, we might get the impression that consciousness plays an important part. It does. "T'ai Chi" is the Supreme Undifferentiated-Absolute, and "Aikido" and "Pa Kua" refer to a harmony of Universal Reality. But how can we form an art of psycho-physical activity on something we can neither see nor touch?

Lift your hand.
How did you lift it?
"I just lifted it."
Who lifted?
"I did."

I don't think I would get much of an argument that you exist, *ergo* "be," or that you appear responsible somehow for the lifting. However, it is perfectly appropriate to question whether this is true or not. You may also want to consider: what is it that is questioning? Thoughts appear to occur, and it appears you read these words, and that process you can neither touch, see, nor hear, but you do not deny it. You simply don't know what it is, and more than likely haven't even questioned it. It may not be what you assume it to be. How is it then that most people either merely believe or don't believe in such distinctions as life force or Being? (Of course everyone believes in "mind" and "self"—are they real?) Who said there was anything to believe in or not? If the name keeps you apart from the issue we're considering, use another name!

Now, let's lift the hand again. Okay, you say you used your mind to lift it; you had the idea and made it happen. But how did you make it happen? You can leave your hand there and "think" about lifting it all day, you can scream and yell, ordering it to rise, but it will not. Not unless something else occurs. Your mind is not directly responsible for the hand lifting. Experience it. What is responsible?

Whatever this "condition" is, it is what we must work with. Being appears as a self, the self appears as body-mind, and what we call "mind" appears as thoughts and feelings. Regardless of any name given, it seems that something translates this conceptual activity into bodily action; this is intent, the energy of mind. Yet, since it moves and takes form in the body, it is also the energy of the body. It is the "force of being alive," the life force. The physical energy of the body tissue itself may ultimately be the same thing, but when we refer to "energy" or "life force" we are usually referring to some occurrence that appears intangible. Wherever the awareness goes, so does the energy. It manifests in objectified relationship, but takes whatever "form" Being directs. This may be one essential meaning of the "Form of Mind."

So Cheng Hsin deals directly with the source and appearance of the activity that we call "mind," and with the occurrence we call "energy." Even though we seem to deal mostly with the body, we are dealing with feeling-awareness also. In performing an action, or learning to do something in a specific way, we must train and work with this "mind and energy," whether we talk about it or not. Many other approaches to what appears to be a similar accomplishment (but which in fact is not) may give results in training, but require no increase in consciousness. Cheng Hsin, on the other hand, is a conscious endeavor. We cannot progress without it.

As I direct your progress, the more you surrender to this and the more conscious you become about what you do, the deeper the changes will be in your body-being. It may well become uncomfortable at times, even in your life as a whole, outside the apparent "doing" of Cheng Hsin. You must have faith and continue; if you are not involved in the process of Consciousness, you are involved in unconsciousness. Tremendous internal discomfort and tremendous joy may both occur, sometimes simultaneously. Other than this work, however, there can only be a quiet suffering, a simple holding-the-line against discomfort, which, in the end, amounts to nothing. These very last remarks are actually made to those more advanced students who have, or will, encounter this dilemma.

Intrinsic strength

The intrinsic strength of the body resides in the inherent binding quality of the tissues. When the tissues of the body are relaxed and alive we have access to these intrinsic qualities, and can use them to achieve an effortless power. We train to align the whole body in this way, and ground the use of intrinsic strength through the feet. This basic idea gives us our motivation and power. In describing this function, I first wrote in personal manuals when I was beginning to discover intrinsic strength (from the oldest manual—1971):

> There is an energy of the body that comes through a mental direction of the feeling-awareness, that moves the mass momentum, and is issued through relaxed limbs. Subject the limbs and upper body to move after this direction, or impulse, is sent from the mass (whole). With practice this can be done on an internal level, or so small that it is difficult to detect, since the limbs are not used (are relaxed), and strength is not obviously used by the muscles.
>
> In using intrinsic strength, keep your spine straight and press on one foot. Bring the other side to move toward the direction of force. Do not try to bend the spine to add back power; this only decreases unity. Allow the body to release into the force, and your mind to be unmoved. Concentrate the idea of power in your lower abdomen, allowing the straight spine

to follow it, and the center to press into one foot. When delivering force, sink into your foot in the same movement, turning your waist as required. The direction of the pelvis is begun as a function of the dropping (sinking) into intrinsic strength, and as the weight is transferred, the completion of the waist, spine, and foot movement occurs—so that the foot then connects with the ground from the dropping into compression, at the moment of impact. Do not try to stand up physically, or tense up at this time. Stay relaxed but full of energy and unity, and hold the idea of dropping (attention, ch'i, strength, etc.) and pressing down. You should concentrate on the lower half, allowing the upper half to rest on and be subject to it. Nurture the breath down into the lower abdomen. Do not be distracted.

Man moves horizontally, but his primary relationship is downward. We forget that the power of the earth is an up-and-down function, and if not for that, no movement would be possible! Horizontal movement gives us freedom, but downward movement gives us power and stability (as well as mobility).

Always use your legs and feet for power, and your center for movement and direction. When your arms are full of ch'i, relaxed and subject to the center, they hit with power but do not feel hard (to you). If you think about hitting hard or with great force, you will inevitably cock and strike out with the shoulder and arm muscles. Although this feels as if it should add strength, it breaks the unity and decreases the power. Realize that for our purposes we use the movement itself, translating earth power (down) into space power (outward), and only the tissues involved minimally in creating that movement should be used, along with sinking and intrinsic strength. All other muscles should be relaxed and all bones (joints) disengaged. Upon hitting or pushing the object, the act is done. No tensing of extra muscles, locking of joints, or pushing out, should occur. So, of course, the pervading idea is one of relaxing. The movement will coordinate and take care of itself by the direction of the feeling-awareness. So a calm mind, relaxing, and whole body view are the places to put the attention, not on power or muscle tension.

The elbows serve to express the hips, so in many cases it is useful to be aware of their functional role. Provided that the waist and legs function correctly, you can put some attention on the elbows to improve your action. In moving and punching, the coordination of the elbows maintains a wholistic body movement. It is as if you pass the connections of the upper body, shoulders and arms (keeping all of those relaxed), and transfer the hip action directly to the elbows, then somehow indirectly to the opponent. Of course you must also maintain proper functional priorities in all parts.

It is important after studying all of the parts to feel your whole body, all together, acting as one unit. You should feel every part from head to toe, and maintain continuous equilibrium and balance.

Although the weight is carried by one foot more than the other, it is best to keep both feet flat and resting on the ground, unless the motion or the functional posture dictate otherwise. The leg, being "full" or weighted and so compressed, is like a rubber ball (tissue) that is filled with air (energy): when you sink into it, it doesn't tense up, but "gives" and catches your weight, compressing naturally, not forcefully. This is the foundation for using intrinsic strength. The whole body has this quality, and as you motivate via the foot and leg, and take this motivation and direct it through the center and hips, the upper body will follow (if you adhere to the body's integration).

By leaving your feeling-attention down with this activity, the energy will get to your hand (or foot, if kicking) spontaneously. But if you raise it and attempt to move the upper on its own, it will segment immediately and destroy the intrinsic value and effortless power. It is this movement—sinking into one foot, relaxing that leg (emptying it and falling into the ground) and shifting the weight to the other leg and compressing it—that is the motivation and power for the center's movement, which in turn directs the rest of the body. Whether moving forward or backward, the feeling-attention is lowered and directed into the feet, and the breath sinks to press the center region, increasing internal pressure, focusing attention on the lower abdomen, and contributing to a centered unity. Most of all relax, and let consciousness direct and unify the feeling-attention so that the body will follow.

A sense of timing and unified actions

When using the lower body for movement, keeping the whole body relaxed, the upper body feels exasperatingly useless! The shoulders do nothing but relax for the most part, and so do the arms. They are so subject to the movement of the whole that it feels as though nothing is happening—but splendidly! It seems that this is a simple process, and it is. It is a freeing and uniting, assigning the proper priorities to all of the functioning elements.

You step forward and strike; your arm is completely relaxed; it feels like nothing at all. Don't try to hit him with power—you'll interfere. Just relax and act. Let me assure you, no exertion of strength is used.

Moving the body in this way will probably feel frustrating at first, but persist. The whole body feeling must act together, as you direct an opening and submission. Sink your energy and attention beneath the floor. Let that be your master!

Need I say more?

About Body-Being transformation

The sets and actions should always be done with the principles in mind. Granted, sometimes it is helpful and necessary to concentrate on one principle or one aspect over others, to do it to extremes in order to understand and incorporate it. Nevertheless, the objective should always be borne in mind: to adhere to all of the points and principles all of the time. When attempting to relax your reactive tendencies and bodily habits in submission to the greater intelligence of Being, you should not "go to sleep" or become "unconscious," but instead increase consciousness, awareness, and aliveness. You should have a vitality and wakefulness, feeling your whole body without tensing up or exerting muscles.

When I say "feel your whole body" I mean literally feel every part! When you put a hand inside a glove, you feel it; where there was just a glove and empty space before, now your hand exists—you have "filled" it. When you feel your body, it is just as real and solid. Fill your foot and leg, pelvis and arms; let no corner or smallest part be unfilled.

However, you must let it be the way that it is. If you think a body part is, or want it to be, a certain way that it is not, you will not be able to fill it. There will be a difference and separation between your self, appearing as an objective condition, and the thought-of-yourself. Like putting a round peg into a square hole, the two won't fit. If you are unwilling to experience "this," then "this" will be denied; you will actively overlook it, be unconscious of it, or ignore it (ignorance). So, even if you want your body to change in a particular way, let it be whatever it is first. After you have filled it, become conscious of it, allowed it to be, you can begin to change it, for now nothing is hidden or denied. Concept and bodily state have become one.

Keep your postures natural. For example, don't turn the hip so far that you twist your knee and break off a solid connection to your feet. Do not twist the knee inward from the toe. Relax the pelvis and learn to create the action within the bounds of weight transference. If you relax the hip joints, the knee should be pushed in the direction of the toe as the pelvis turns, not pulled in the direction of the turning.

It is by understanding the limits of movement that we can obtain real freedom in movement. By moving within these bounds we can relax and move freely and completely, without running into binding limitations, or having to "check" our movement to keep from losing balance. When we want to change, or move elsewhere, we simply shift the bounds.

> *Expression is form. Knowing the nature of the limits of form allows us to create a full expression within that condition. Therefore, we see that form is not rigid and has no necessity or meaning in itself. It must be created and changed as appropriate to the situation and purpose at hand. Adhering to the event and function in this moment allows real freedom of expression.*

Posture

Of course, to fulfill the demands of functional interaction, the body must be in a proper state: constantly relaxed, balanced, answering to the dictates of ever-shifting forces, and maintaining alignment to the principles and points I've mentioned about body-being. In these arts the body must have a certain roundness as well as a certain angularity to it. There must be a harmony and development to its lines and curves. Not only must they be unified, but the geometric patterns that are developed must be interrelated and complementary within themselves, as well as responsive to the whole and the qualities of outside force.

The bodily state is continually changing. That is why it is imperative to be in touch with the constant principles that are unchanged and, at the same time, the source or foundation of change. It is alignment to these principles that enables us to respond completely, so that one response does not block or deter the next. If the body, mind, and energy do not adhere to this, every move will detract from real equilibrium, and errors will accumulate with every response.

Relaxation is the key to effective function in both body and mind. If the mind is not calm throughout, the body will not respond correctly or magically.

Of course, adherence to the functional priorities is essential to maintaining correct posture during activity. When we respond rather than react, we can use the lower over the upper and inner over the outer. If we react at all, however, the reverse will be the case, disrupting our connection with the earth, our body, and energy. Feeling-attention will be tied up in the current of reactive emotion and muscular tension, and therefore unavailable to us.

To think that the posture of the physical body is the only priority is superficial, but to think that only energy and mind development are important, disregarding the "mere physical," is a grave mistake. Everything we do manifests itself through the physical, and thus in the posture; what is done, in a sense, is "posture." Posture is the tool of function, as function is the tool of understanding. How separate can one be from another? To relax the body, sink feeling and attention, and respond appropriately *is* mind and energy. Consciousness "dictates" movement and function. And it is also the body. Body "does" movement and function. They are inseparable!

In its own way posture is a complete study. The body is the posture. The energy has posture, too. How the energy moves, unifies and balances is the energy's posture, and totally affects the physical posture. Mind has posture also; we want to adhere to a mind posture that is calm and perceptive. It is obvious that none of these postures can be separated. When we do anything, all must be included. Posture must be part of our present consciousness and cannot be forgotten, even though we must be conscious of all other things as well. This awareness is not necessarily easy to achieve and maintain, for it demands that we remain conscious of it all, and all at once. It is the only way.

The source of posture must be recognized in order to create appropriate and functional postures as changing situations demand. The posture comes from the position adopted or generated by Being. It is visibly affected by attitude, emotional orientation, and conceptualizations. The idea must not be one of adopting a pose or style in movement, nor of what the posture appears like; rather, it is in keeping to the principles. Thus the Classics state: "Essentially everything depends solely on Consciousness and not on external appearance." To give up trying to accomplish results by use of muscular force or intellect and letting all depend on the Principles of Being *(Hsin)* is posture done correctly.

Functional mind

It is important to understand the difference between **reaction** and **response**. A response is born of calm mind and sensitive awareness. It is accurate and emerges from a state of equilibrium and balance. It is not blocked or forced and occurs spontaneously, with no fear, desire or consideration, but with great intelligence and "in-tunement." What is needed and appropriate simply occurs.

A reaction, however, is the antithesis of a response, although both are involved in activity and relationship. A reaction is born of urges and tendencies, and of unconsciousness, separative viewpoint, and unstable mind. It is oppressed by fears, desires, and considerations prior to and following its appearance. When it occurs, it is a blind thrashing of the unconscious tendency toward protection. Reaction is contractive in nature. It is a withdrawal of sensitivity and relational awareness to act, often in a negative fashion, in an attempt to solve or end (destroy) the apparent source of immediate danger or dilemma. There is no real participation in or responsibility for that act, and no real sense of what is appropriate. A reaction is not geared to continuation. Each is a one-shot attempt to save oneself; an expression that stems from of a sense of demanding urgency to be protected, founded on a feeling of inadequacy to accomplish this task responsibly.

In combat, use their reactive force.

Reactive tendencies are not always violent or sudden, but they seem always to involve a deep sense of fear and dilemma. They are, by nature, heartless and not based on the moment, but emotionally bound to the past and recoiling from the future. Although safety and security are the motivating factors in reactive tendency, the reaction itself often tends to involve more suffering and imbalance (therefore danger) than no action at all. The inharmonious relationship between self and situation is often made worse. When a conflict seems to have been resolved by reaction, most often it is a postponement, not a resolution, and the real cost has not yet been realized. Of course, sometimes a reaction appears to have "saved the day." However, this is the exception, and cannot be counted on; furthermore, we must clearly distinguish between a fast response and a reaction.

The essence of the distinction between these two lies mostly in the quality and state of mind. If an action is free from fear and obsessive desire (and I do not mean free from feeling fear or having desire; I mean not bound to, motivated by, or influenced by them), and receptive to the real condition; and, most importantly, if the mind and energy are not disturbed or disrupted in any way by the stimulus that calls for action; then it is responsive. Thus, if the stimulus does not call for action, no action is taken; whereas a reaction occurs whether action is called for or not. In reacting we can feel the energy disturbed, the mind upset and the unconscious quality of the act being made. By design, reactions are general, not specific to the immediate situation; they act as a closure to (whether moving toward or away from) what appears. They tend to be a one-fits-all relationship to what's occurring.

Lead him to collide with himself; move when he is halfway between one act and another, and have his reaction collide with his action!

When thoughts and feelings are non-reactive, calm, and responsive only, then the posture may become natural and remain natural in the midst of activity. Within responsiveness your body-being returns continuously to the natural condition, never leaving equilibrium, and becoming still as soon as activity is not called for. In this way the body remains intact, whole, relaxed, and always open to respond; you are not recoiling internally, have no wave of resistance and are not "floating," or severed from your groundedness. Maintaining this condition of relaxed balance and postural integration is as delicate as it is effective. On one level, it is like blinking when something flashes towards your eyes. The root lies in that urge to react, not in the activity itself. Don't try to stop the act; merely remove the urge, then no act will arise.

Use a quiet and patient Heart to direct actions of destruction.

A precious word about function

Increase your sensitivity to the opponent's state and intentions. When you feel a reaction or impulse of resistance in the opponent, due to apprehension, loss of balance, mental or energy disturbance, resistance, or confusion (bodily or otherwise), adjust your weight and alignment to utilize this reactive resistance, but do not tense your limbs in any way. When pressure is applied the thought should be in the center region, and in the correct movement of the pelvis and legs. The feeling-awareness will move to the arms by itself; feeling-impulse will direct the body's activity simply through sensitivity to the opponent's state, but you must not create tension in the limbs.

> Let the opponent mold his own defeat, as you are free to be molded.

When the attention resides in the lower abdomen, and the feeling-awareness presses into the foot to create the intrinsic strength, the arms must be made to relax and rely on the movement itself to produce the result, and not on tension. Effectiveness in these processes is essential to success with the functional or interactive "powers," or energies. Among these powers are: **following, borrowing, contributing,** and **joining**. The names indicate the nature of the principle involved. I will discuss this more fully later.

Here is one of the most accurate and encompassing statements I've made about skillful interaction:

> My actions are not my own, but follow the way of the environment. I do not try, but step here or there and let the outcome occur.

To do this is a beautiful feeling.

Increase conscious sensitivity so that a "fly cannot alight, nor a feather be added." Although only one part may be touched, all parts are responsive. The pressure applied to any part is accepted by the whole, for every joint is open and all parts relaxed and unified. Borrow his force and energy to move your own body, sticking mentally and/or physically to his every action. Adjust your hips and legs so that you never let more than a few ounces touch you. Yielding is the objective, and it must also be continuous. The more you yield the harder it may become, for you are then forced to give up your will and be imposed upon for so long. This tendency will be dissolved when you learn to cling less, and make change your principle.

Constantly change into the appropriate action from moment to moment.

By becoming conscious of the context for his intent and strategy —reading his mind, so to speak—you will be able to follow your opponent's movements. Observe that to which he is bound and you will know what he will do.

Watch the water, not the fish. See the road he is on and you will know which way he must turn.

By turning with him you can easily follow and evade, and naturally take advantage. It is by receiving him with no fear and nothing to protect that he becomes yours. You must let him in, consciously and physically, and the energies must merge; then the mind will understand and the feeling-impulse will respond. Your "force of being" then fills out and is complete, without the slightest resistance.

In pursuit of Being (Hsin)

What is the "form" of your mind? What shape is it? What color, size, or qualities does it have? Experience it. Become conscious of whatever may be the case. It may not exist at all!

Not-Knowing is the original or fundamental condition of Being.

The framework within which we direct the feeling-awareness, or life force, is one way of considering the "form" of being alive. For example, if our feeling-attention is aligned at every moment with the Principles and points mentioned in this book, our mind will be wholly occupied by this way of being. Therefore, within the distinction that we call the psycho-physical, the "form" the mind and energy take is how we direct the "force" of being alive.

This "mind-self" is found in all of our activities; all that we do is affected by conceptualization or interpretation. Our physical actions are a direct result of the "force of being" as activity, and therefore reveal the life force, which includes the activity we call "mind." When I move here, or relax this, you then "see" my mind moving, or "appearing." The more understanding, feeling, and true direction of every aspect of our actions that we obtain, the more accurate and truly representative our actions are, becoming the appearance of *creative* activity. So what occurs within the body, its activity, and the relationships that are evolving and changing as a result, is a reflection of the phenomenon we call mind.

Whatever its nature, it is this "condition" with which we must work. But if we are powerless to change this principle condition, what difference does it make if we become conscious of it or not? Before I direct myself to that question, let me clarify the fact that mere "participation" in anything does not endow the participant with principle insight into the nature of the event in which he is participating. Thus, we may not be able to change this "essential condition," but we can change our relationship to it. I will use a story as an analogy.

A man has spent his life terrified to move anywhere, for when he does he invariably experiences great pain. Driven to survive, he is forced to move anyway. Suddenly he is struck with a sharp pain; sensitivities frayed, he reacts blindly with terror, and sure enough, his flesh is torn and ripped and he is reduced to a horrible condition. His life is a hell, and his best moments and highest accomplishments occur when he does nothing and achieves nothing, being comfortable with the absence of pain. But still he suffers in the knowledge that eventually he must move again to survive. This is his condition. However, one day someone comes along and turns on a light (one that happened to be available all the time). At that instant, the man realizes for the first time that all along he has been in the dark, and he now sees that he is standing in the middle of a rose garden! Now it is a simple and clear matter for him to avoid the thorns, and to move freely and openly; he even has a world of beautiful roses to smell, see, and enjoy everywhere he looks!

The condition around him is exactly the same. Nothing has changed except his ability to see it, to become conscious of it. However, his entire life activity, his approach and relationship to it, even his abilities and accomplishments, have all changed radically. This realization was not just a casual understanding; an intellectual knowledge of his condition would have served him little. He needed the "light," the real and present consciousness of this condition—

not as a memory, but as a constant and present experience.

We must be willing to experience whatever may be the case. If any part of ourselves is unwilling to experience and open up to any possibility, conceivable or not, we won't. It is our endeavor to become directly conscious of this very "condition" of Being. "Willingness to experience" occasions the absence of fear. This allows an increase in real attention and open Presence. In our life as well as our art we are then able to evade the thorns and pluck the rose!

Chapter Four

The Cheng Hsin Body-Being
A Further Description

On the nature of energy

When first adapting to the principle that I mentioned in the section on designing or creating an opening to use intrinsic strength (the main notion being "hand up—you down"), it feels as if the energy falls downward, away from our goal or object of function. Actually, this is necessary because we have confused energy use with its binding control or containment. It is like opening valves that exist along a water line; if the valves are closed, the water does not flow. The more open they are, the more flow we achieve, and each valve gets larger and releases more water the further down we go. We have confused the use of the water (energy) with the contraction of the valves. Thus, we use the "pipe" to attempt function, rather than the "water." The nature of energy is that it wants to flow, so when we close the valves to its flow, we get pressure or tension. This produces the "sensation" of strength, which is how we have learned to "use" energy. But this accomplishment is indirect, using the "pressure" of energy through the vehicle of its function.

Energy (ch'i or life force) is not felt directly as something; it is felt as a function, as a relational manifestation. The changes that occur to allow it to be "used"—which may look like creating a flow, channeling its direction, or the things that are "touched" and made conscious (tissues, nerves, air, etc.) are the ways that we "know" energy. Although the use of energy is not dependent on

53

the sensation of contraction, its primary quality is some form of feeling. This "feeling" is what energy does; it is not the energy itself. In the beginning, we must feel things and direct this feeling; if we do not feel, we are not moving energy. As we open, the feelings become more subtle and fine; eventually we develop access to it as created experience, which is more direct or closer to the source of what energy "is," than a sensation of feeling. Since we are attempting a transformation of the gross reactive tendencies in energy use, we must first move into dynamic feeling changes to achieve transition. (Do not try to bypass this!) Therefore, the real feeling of draining the very "substance" of the body down into the earth is the necessary unlocking and opening, relaxing and "plugging into," that which will allow the energy to flow. This flow will at first be less noticeable than the draining.

I want to draw two distinctions that appear in and as the "force" of things. These distinctions appear as principles of what occurs, and so can be seen whenever something "is," or is moving (activity). I want to use an analogy that may clarify and make useful what I'm considering here. These two distinctions I call the **great forces**, and can be artificially and symbolically likened to fire and water.

What we are talking about are two dynamic forces. One is that which solidifies, unifies, connects and includes. This is the order of that which tends down, since "down" is what appears in our relation to the earth. Gravity could be seen as exemplifying this force; intrinsic strength, which in the case of our body is the inherent binding quality of the tissues, is another example of this distinction. Understanding the true nature of this distinction, we see that intrinsic strength and gravity are ultimately the same force. I'm symbolizing this distinction with water.

The other distinction is the natural force of expansion, radiance, release, and the like. Awareness and energy extension are thus related to this force. Again, in our relationship to the earth we might see it as a tendency to rise, but this is only because it appears contrary to the draw toward unification. This is not so. Its tendency is expansion, inclusive of that which goes down; we simply notice it only when it goes up or out. I'm symbolizing this with fire.

Actually, there is no clear-cut natural example of one or the other of these forces, since they both appear in everything. We merely make the distinction and then apply it for the sake of con-

sideration to a quality or thing. These distinctions are totally relational, and so do not exist "on their own." As a matter of fact,
they are not even different forces, but the same event. Yet it is the
very possibility out of which they act as if distinct, and our perception of them as distinct, that allows for things to appear to "be."

When we consider the design of the event in which we appear,
there seems to be the possibility of balance between these forces
and the possibility of imbalance. The possibility of imbalance is
actually only activity, which is to say an interplay of the forces, so
that movement takes place (this activity itself might be seen as the
force of expansion). In the case of imbalance this activity is simply the
reestablishment of balance (which is itself seen as stillness). However, for our purpose we wish to establish a balance and activity
that fall within the parameters of our own welfare. For this we
need to coordinate and align our body structure and movement to
these forces so that a constant balance between them is maintained.

Using the symbolic analogue I established: water tends downward and is more solid and tangible than fire; aside from its heat,
fire is easily perceived as intangible. (Heat is not a necessary quality
of expansion, although it is a frequent one.) When we allow the
water energy to follow its nature, and the fire energy to follow its
nature, all is well. When the water goes down, the fire may rise.
If we "hold" the water up, as seen in not relaxing and not grounding, the fire cannot fulfill its function, and vice versa. We have
confused our relationship with these two forces as one of control,
pitting the "fire" against the "water" and creating contraction.

To correct many of the tendencies that draw our body-being
into disharmony or imbalance, I would like to recommend the
following. In our body when some part, and associated parts, lift
upward or outward, we must direct and feel an inward and downward draining, so that the energy may flow freely. Once this is
done we can allow ourselves free expression, letting the feeling of
flow extend across the room in a line, fill the room as a whole, or
manifest itself in any way we wish, and it will be backed up by
the "ground" for the energy—its counterpart, so to speak.

Since we are life, and it is a function of life to operate with
both great forces (Union and Expansion) we are, in a sense, caught
between the two. I have called this experience "being caught between
heaven and earth." Living beings are always in this condition, for
without one force or the other, life would not exist. We mistakenly

and habitually adapt to our perceived relationship to these forces. Operating from a sense of separateness and limitation, we adjust ourselves to the force of Union, of settling, of coming together, as contraction into our body-self with awareness, tension and attitude. Similarly, our relationship to the force of Expansion, expression, communication and creativity, has become one of manipulation, excessive "doingness," and "infliction" (whether the known attitude is one of goodness or badness).

Therefore, it becomes more apparent to us why, on so many levels, we adopt either resistance or force. We are operating from such a limited sense of body-self that expansion becomes forcing and union becomes resistance. Our adaptation in Cheng Hsin, however, entails transformation or surrender to the greater forces of Union (Inclusion) (adopting an attitude of acceptance, responsive receptance, using intrinsic strength or effortless power and relaxing into the earth, for example) and Expansion (answering to the flow and demands of movement and forces, being three-dimensional, and extending awareness). The points of marrow-draining (hand up—you down) and energy flow (energy extension) purposefully adhere to this principle.

On the adaptation to the great force known as Inclusion

This is one of the fundamental qualities of the functioning Cheng Hsin Body-Being. It represents one of the three principal aspects of the state of body-being achieved in Cheng Hsin.

Briefly, alignment with the principle of inclusion or union— what I figuratively named the "water" principle—requires the surrender of our body-being to the earth and its power. Once this is accomplished, the energy received from alignment with the earth then feeds the body as power, which is felt at times as a force moving upward. This process involves each of the great forces in a specific way, but our attention is directed primarily toward relaxing into and alignment with the earth. This force may be perceived as a downward flow, since the earth is the most massive and central force relative to us.

One way to draw our attention, and thus our energy and alignment, into a direct accommodation to the force of "union," is to adopt some objective relational feeling-image. This feeling-image must already be fully and naturally aligned with the force or principle with which we want to bring our being into direct alignment. Two feeling-images that serve to bring the body into alignment with this principle are the "ball and chain" and the "water-drop."

The ball and chain simply refers to the feeling-image of a one-thousand-pound lead ball hanging beneath the ground and between your feet, attached to your center with a chain. With such a feeling-image, the force or draw of union to the earth becomes actively apparent, as well as the demand to align the body structure to it. I think you'll find that this alignment will be complementary and/or identical to the eight points on posture that I mentioned earlier.

To create the water-drop feeling-image, feel beneath the ground the equivalent distance of the distance from the ground to the center. In order to do this, first notice that space extends beneath your feet. It may be filled with earth, yet distance does exist in that direction. Now you can begin to feel it, having acknowledged its existence. Feel the space in between and around the legs, like a half-sphere that is resting on the ground, the top of which passes through your center. This space should come to feel as if the air within it is fuller and thicker than normal, and should be equally strong and balanced in all directions.

The other half of this sphere is under the ground. Fill that space with your "life force" through the conceptual presence of the water-drop, which then both gives and draws your feeling-attention. Remember that the water-drop is equally full on all sides, so that no matter which way you move or turn, it remains central and balanced. This drops your sense of location to a much lower position than usual, and allows you to operate from there, feeding off of the alignment to the earth.

Above the sphere, from the head to the center in a vertically descending fall line, is the top of the water-drop shape. It starts from a point at the crown and flares out equally as it falls until it hits the center region; there it engulfs the center-pelvic area and blends with the large sphere discussed above. It is this inverted top that flows into the lower sphere (draining of deep tension).

The value of adherence to this felt imagery is manifold. Much greater power is achieved through the use of intrinsic strength, and through a more direct connection with the alignment that this

adaptation represents. Stability, centeredness, calmness, groundedness, fullness or three-dimensional balance, and even speed; all
arise from this condition.

In order to make full functional use of the water-drop, you
must learn to move it and allow it in turn to move your body.
Begin by feeling the area around your legs and under your feet.
Then, feel this area move in the direction that you wish, as if the
very substance of space moves, and allow that feeling to move
your body from the legs and pelvis.

You must feel this image as a "reality," even though it is formed
through conceptualization. To be effective it must be perceived,
felt, as "real," existing as a "presence,"—one with the qualities
we're looking for, and so one that draws out or gives being to the
relational disposition that those qualities elicit.

Our attitudes and sense of our own relational condition to
things will change as a function of and in alignment to this new
way of holding your energy. It may seem superficial to surrender
to something that we apparently create. Nevertheless, although
our conceptualization (which is not limited to mere abstraction)
determines the space and qualities that our energy occupies, it
does not "create" the energy. It is itself in the field that is the
"force of being alive," (life force or energy at its source), and so
we could say that it is through energy that our conceptualization
appears, or arises from Being. The energy is the source of our
activity; and Being as Consciousness (not to be confused with the
mind or what you "know") is the source of that energy. Therefore,
we must continue to surrender to the life force and let it govern
our actions. When the life force occupies conditions that align
with the forces that are, it is functionally much more powerful.
The water-drop is such a manifest condition; so, although we conceptualize it, we are actually letting our energy fulfill a natural
adaptation. We must surrender our impulse-to-action to the principles of Being and the feeling-images we use to align with them.
This process must be held and felt conceptually until our habit to
do otherwise is fully adapted and aligned to the design that is.

From this depth of alignment we receive the power of the
design of Being that is the event of being human, since we are
connected with and surrendered to it. This event is shaped by the
principles of three-dimensionality (space) and mass (objects). Relative to us, the earth and air (or space) are the primary representa-

tions of these two principles, and will consequently bestow "power" upon anyone who surrenders his separateness relative to these principles. Thus, stability, wholeness, and groundedness are necessary qualities that accompany alignment to these principles.

We may attain many of the points and qualities of the Cheng Hsin Body-Being by adopting states such as the water-drop, since these qualities are inherent in the water-drop. Such an adaptation allows sinking (water-drops fall down), calmness (putting the mind in the center and surrendering to a lower position), relaxing (draining downward and allowing the power to be of the earth, frees the tissue from tension and allows the energy to flow), unity, aligning with gravity, a natural use of intrinsic strength (and its ready availability), functional priorities, and many other qualities. This is why states of energy like the water-drop are invaluable tools for alignment with the Cheng Hsin Body-Being.

Absolute presence in objectified reality

This state of being is an adaptation to Expansion, the second of the two great forces. Both the water-drop and absolute presence are only tools for our adaptation to the great forces, and each is inclusive of both forces. However, the water-drop primarily embodies aspects of the principle of centralization and inclusion, or consolidation and union, which is often seen in our body-being as an inward and downward flow. Conversely, we tend to see absolute presence as representative of expansion, totality and radiance, apparently flowing upward and outward. However, notice that union is equal to totalness; expansion is equal to inclusion; and center to radiance. We only identify direction as a point of view.

Absolute presence is really a more extensive look at the Eight-Attitude Awareness. In establishing your relationship to this, review experientially the awareness I called the Eight Attitudes. Be sure to fill out on all sides and in all places, leaving no hole or lopsidedness. Practice making the space around your body thicker or more densely filled with your life force (energy, feeling) and extended out in all directions. As you do this, make sure that the extent and density you establish on any side or area is equalled by all other sides. If you feel very full and expansive toward your front, for example, be sure your rear is equally full and equally extensive. If it is not, then spend more time putting energy into that area.

Check that down, up, inside, and all other relations are equal.

Besides the force or principle of Expansion, we must consider the principle manifest in three-dimensional space. Allowing our feeling-attention to fill out the entire three-dimensional space that our body occupies as an objective mass, and the three-dimensional space in which it abides and is so defined, aligns us to this principle. Our thinking, activity and awareness will then accommodate this principle, and every relational action will be more effective.

If we notice that this presence also extends down we see that it includes the water-drop space. In the Eight Attitudes, that which does not exist is a part of our awareness. At first, we may relate to this suggested form of conceptualization as simply another idea or technique. However, some states are more aligned to the event that we hold as "reality" than others, and so are much more powerful—more useful, functional, or workable. Entering what is presently occurring is what allows power to become available, since all form exists and is directed by the life force and the life force abides only in the present. Establishing absolute presence is a function of allowing the life force to be full, occupying the condition of form that is immediate, raw and untouched by our assessment of it. From this state whatever we do will be more powerful.

Since Being or Consciousness does not occupy space or time, we must also abide in that which does not exist in order to be with that which creates and directs the life force. Although Consciousness occupies no time or space, it manifests via the life force in the Present. Therefore, adaptation to this Absolute Presence in reality is much more than a technique, and demands a process of psycho-physical transformation.

On the Intrinsic Force of the Body-Being

Energy and matter are essentially the same, but manifest differently. All things, including the tissues of the body, have an inherent binding quality, an intrinsic strength of their own. We can use this intrinsic physical quality, tap it in our own bodies, by continuously flowing into the gravitational pull and working with the pressure created by sinking into the planet. However, this is only possible through the direction of feeling-awareness or intention, and is only powerful when done with a wholeness in our conceptualization; therefore awareness and intention also represent an aspect of internal power.

The energy that we feel in and around the body, feeling in general, and adoption of any particular state or conceptualized energy form, also appear to be qualities intrinsic to human psycho-physical existence. Our ability to create states or invent objectified qualities in our life force, as well as to notice the existing energy flows and conditions, increases our power manifold. The very source of the body-being, which is the force or power of being alive, action, impulse, volition, thinking and feeling, *is* the intrinsic nature of a living body, or *being alive*. Aligning with that force of being puts us at that source, a position of effortless power.

> *There is an inverse proportion of pressure needed to the amount and quality of energy-attention applied to produce a result. Combine and use all factors at once.*

Being conscious of the real present condition, and what it takes to affect it appropriately, is a real internal power. This is not an abstraction, however, but a very real, direct feeling-perception; and all actions, such as feeling, awareness and body movement, must arise accordingly.

> *Understand that 'Intrinsic Force' is the connective or binding quality of all things—the attraction separation has for union.*

Of course, internal power goes beyond the mind, and beyond our ability to perceive with our intellect or common perceptions what it is or how it works. Nevertheless, the life force, which essentially *is* all internal power and life itself, works regardless of our intellectual grasp of it.

An exercise of the life force

As you can see, a large part of this kind of training is actually an exercise and training of the **life force**. Life force—the force of life, or what appears as Being—is inherent in all of the forms that arise as a function of our activities, such as thinking, feeling, moving, perceiving, emoting, and so on. Whatever we wish to do, we must do it via the life force. Therefore, putting our whole feeling-attention into the space and objects, action, and stillness (including that of our own body and mind), that are our immediate involvement in the present, is always the beginning of exercising the life force.

This is totally inclusive of all of the space and objects around us. We must feel them as well as be aware of them in order to participate fully in the present moment. This practice is the basic exercise of the life force, and empowers all other training.

Have no 'dead' life force.

Training the life force is similar to training the body; we must exercise it to make it stronger, more vital and more readily usable and plastic. The more concretely and quickly we can adopt feeling and conceptual qualities in our body-being, the greater our ability to use the life force.

It is our ability to use the life force that determines our ability to adapt to the great forces. It is the appropriate blend and balance between these two principal forces with our life force that allow us all of what we call internal powers and skills, even such abilities as listening or using feeling-states to affect another's energy.

Study, contemplation and practice

To pursue any multi-dimensional field of study to the depth that we do in Cheng Hsin, we need a multi-dimensional approach. I make three important distinctions in this approach. These are **study, practice,** and **contemplation**. Each approach should be given equal attention, for all three are necessary for rapid growth and development.

Study is the "food" for understanding. It entails reading, discussing and considering what's read; observing and learning about particular aspects of movement; reviewing, taking apart and thinking about your movements, relationships and frustrations; and consciously incorporating the principles in their extreme into what you do. Basically, it is questioning and dwelling upon, taking apart and observing, considering, examining, and discovering what is at hand.

Practice is the "ground" for understanding and development. It encompasses the active development, necessary training, and "undoing." Practice includes doing your movements and techniques while adhering to the principles; engaging in any ritual practice, such as *t'ui shou*; free and active play, such as free fighting; or working on and repeating techniques, or "energies." "Internal" development (working with the force of being alive) must be cultivated and repeatedly practiced as well. It is the activity of transfiguration in the body-being.

Contemplation is the "source" of understanding and possibly its absorption. I define contemplation as "being open to a direct experiential breakthrough in consciousness with the intent that it occur." It is presently putting all feeling-attention on a question, and throwing yourself completely open to the possibility of experiencing the truth of the matter, without preconception or preference. This is done as a discipline, without force or avoidance and without being distracted.

Meditation might come under this category, yet I see meditation as more of a cultivation of desired qualities, like open-stillness, clarity and calmness of mind, or engaging the "force of being alive" in a healing process. Practically speaking, contemplation could be seen as a total concentration of your feeling-attention on truly asking a question continually and with openness for a period of time. It is not "figuring out" (that is for study); it is more a matter of allowing the obvious understanding, breakthrough, or realization to arise or become conscious, by allowing the question to permeate the body and Being until this occurs.

Here is where study and practice are useful. For example, the "frustration" we feel during a practice or study session can be the object of such a contemplation. When we are frustrated there is obviously something we desire to have happen that is being thwarted. It is almost a certainty that there is something being ignored. It is in this ignorance, then, that the possibility of a solution lies. So if our question is along the lines of: "How do I interact such that it turns out?" then it must also be: "With what am I to interact?" This latter question compels us to face whatever is being ignored. We begin by letting the frustration be with us, and basically "sit with it" until it becomes a real and active part of our present experience. Then, without too much mental probing, we allow our "mindless" intelligence to reveal what is being ignored—and therefore to achieve the solution to the frustration.

In one sense we can say that we have total freedom of movement in concepts, assumptions, feeling, and "imagined" body. With this freedom we can correct or recognize the limitations of our objective through the intuitive understanding of a natural process we already possess. However, when I say "imagined" body, I do not mean intellectually so. It must be accurately and definitively felt as real. Increased practice and study help to realize this by making body-feel and energy awareness more acute and familiar. However, this specific technique borders on study, so you must discern for yourself what is needed from moment to moment.

In any case, study, practice and contemplation should all be done equally and interdependently as part of one process.

The Cheng Hsin symbol

The Cheng Hsin symbol represents alignment with the design and principles of the event of Being.

The inner circular form represents the principle of inclusion. In our body-being we align to the principle of union or inclusion by centering our feeling-attention and, by draining downward, making a connection with the earth. The outer circle represents the principle of expansion, or radiance into the whole, total, and equally balanced energy all around our body-being in awareness, referring back to the totality of the absolute presence. Thus, it symbolizes the principle of expansion. The break in the circle at the top is a symbolic reference to Being, and thus the greater power and intelligence that is the source of our being. We train to allow this to govern all of our actions. In the symbol we also see that the inner and outer, the female and male, inclusion and expansion are joined, and are actually the same event, in the coming together that represents Being.

Within this basic alignment to these fundamental principles, we can adopt an infinite variety of relational forms and activities, and give being to whatever needs to appear. It includes all that is existence and non-existence. Therefore, the Cheng Hsin symbol represents the two fundamental principles and Being (*Hsin* or source), relative to our body-self as the point of reference.

Chapter Five

An Introduction
to Functional Considerations

T his section brings into consideration the question of an appropriate state of being to adopt in functional interaction. So we must look into the relationship that we have with ourselves, and the relationship that we have with others. Since the event of being a self appears multi-dimensionally, we can well imagine that interaction and relationship between selves will be an even greater affair. For skill to arise, all that appears to be must be included and harmonized within the functional interaction.

Therefore, we are looking for something which may be complex or multi-dimensional, yet is simply and functionally occurring all the time, and in every moment. It must represent the fundamental principles of action, perception and cognition, and be the state of being that accomplishes what we wish to develop in Cheng Hsin. It is useful to see that various activities (such as the distinctions found in the "following energies" in which one may appear to be used more than another at any particular moment, thus appearing to come and go) are actually representations of the same event and come from the same root. In this way we can abide in a position of being that includes all activity regardless of what appears to come and go. By so doing we can establish a "state" of being that can functionally and appropriately meet events as they arise.

This section is founded on everything stated in previous chapters, and so everything reviewed is done so on a deeper level and demands an even more profound attention and understanding.

It should immediately become obvious that many of these functional considerations are in fact similar in nature to the Five Principles. This is true because they come from these principles. It is not an easy task to achieve the State of Being that is considered in these next chapters. It demands a great deal of attention and study. Furthermore, it demands experience and breakthrough. It must become your experience in understanding, and your experience in bodily state and activity. Some points demand more attention to body and energy; some depend more upon intention and awareness. They all demand "experiential-understanding," or insight. However, once this state is achieved you may enter into a realm that needs no defense and you may freely manifest the skill and function that is the heart of our practice.

The first thing you must do is adopt the proper attitude in approaching what is to follow. That attitude has to be one of "not-knowing." Whatever you know is fine; put it aside. Open yourself to not knowing and remain that way while looking at and experiencing these points.

You need never formulate a belief or a conclusion as to what these things mean or are. You only have to stay open and in a state of "not-knowing." The experience of any given point, or all points, that create the complete state of Being, is the only thing that should emanate from this not-knowing; that is the "knowing." So you need never attempt to "fill" not-knowing. The point is simply to experience what is presented here, not to know it. In that way it becomes a profound understanding, totally full and complete, without any holes whatsoever.

The Cheng Hsin Four Principles of Function

Once again, although we will consider several distinctions in the fundamental aspects of functional ability, the One-Principle should be sought out. However, this will be next to impossible without some experiential understanding of the distinctions. I have made four distinctions in what appears as functional ability. They are based on the principles that allow ability to occur. As with the principles of body-being, the "principles of function" are not really the *principles* themselves; they are instead four principal distinctions in ability attained. In other words, once being is aligned to the principles that allow ability to occur, the "state"—or activity of being—that arises can be seen in these four distinctions.

These four "principles" of function are listening, outreaching, joining, and neutralizing. Like the principles of body-being, these represent an alignment with the principles that are, rather than an expression of the principle itself. Eventually in our studies this understanding should be pursued, since it is only from the principle itself that any creativity can arise in relation to that principle.

I have called these the four principles of function because of their central and essential position in functional ability and skill. They are also far-reaching in form of application and extrapolation. These four are actually done all at once, and are seen as elements to functionality. Although technical training and competence are necessary, without these principles applied to and founding the techniques, they will not be Cheng Hsin, nor will our ability move beyond randomness in workability.

Listening

Listening has been discussed in various forms; it is all that you do to perceive, sense, or "get in touch with," whatever is occurring. You can listen to, be aware of, and feel your own body, any part of it or the whole, as well as the particular way all parts relate, align, or connect. Listening applies to being sensitive, in the present moment, of your own energy currents, energy states, mental states and feeling states. Of course, you must listen to, perceive and feel all these in another, from his (her) whole body to his energy currents and thoughts. You must also begin to pick up on how he "holds the world," and thus see his limitations and strengths. In such a moment, you also see outside his limitations and beyond his strengths and can deal with him accordingly.

Acceptance of what is, or may be, is always the first step.

Listening includes maintaining awareness and energy three-dimensionally, in and around the body, as well as perception or "in-touchness" of the entire present relational condition in this very moment. It is knowing what is happening, being aware of what is occurring.

Outreaching

Outreaching refers to actually "touching" or making a connection with all that you perceive through Listening. I describe outreaching as connecting with, or touching, your whole body, the ground, and another's whole body. This should be done on a "Being" level, a feeling (energy) level, and a physical level, usually all three at once. For example, when I'm touching someone physically, I am outreaching if I am connected directly to his or her entire body, and I feel this. I include and touch or "feel" his energy currents and intention and, through my whole body, connect both of us with the ground. Outreaching isn't restricted to physical contact, however; it can and should also be done without touch. It is simply making a feeling-connection with what is occurring, be it with physical contact or without. In outreaching you are engaging the life force and allowing a direct connection between this feeling impulse and our interpreted experience of what's occurring, which, as a whole, is translated into a feeling form so that the body can relate to it directly.

> *Detect and feel his whole body; penetrate to his center and feet; touch his balance and reactivity; locate his intent and impulse to act.*

Joining

Joining is blending or appropriately interacting with what is "touched" in outreaching. It is activity based on an appropriate interpretation of all relational factors. As such, joining is activity that is totally and purposefully commensurate with the activity of the other or the event. Joining is producing a result within the context of following. Following represents commensurate action to what is occurring, such that all arising activity, if it presents an imbalancing effect, is both neutralized and followed, so that you are constantly adjusting into an advantageous relationship as changes occur. This can be done in many ways, some of which are found in the four powers yet to be discussed. It can also be seen as running your "energy" currents into the opponent's in a blending or joining fashion. Listening and outreaching must be done continuously, as they are fundamental to and inherent in what I call joining. To comprehend joining, from which all techniques spring, you must understand the proper use of expansion and inclusion.

> *Joining is a calm activity, with both parties helping each other defeat the aggressor.*

Whenever the body comes into physical contact with anything, it must be allowed to compress. This compression occurs without effort and as a function of intrinsic strength, the binding force that is already present in the tissues of the body. It must also make an unbroken connection from the point of contact to the ground, effortlessly and in proper alignment, so that the intrinsic quality of the body can be used.

At the same time, an outreaching flow of feeling-attention or "energy" expands to touch and include the other. This energy is the same force that moves the body. A sensitive feeling-attention aligns the body, "sets it up" and drops it into place, with the proper timing and at the proper distance, so that the intrinsic qualities of the tissues can be used. The energy is not held trapped in the tissue; rather, it is allowed to run free, and the body, not bound by tension, is free to follow this energy.

Joining combines all that has been mentioned in this book thus far, as well as considerations of timing, geometry, distances, spatial relationships, states of being, physics and psychology. It is the functional base from which we create all of our techniques.

Neutralizing

When in Danger—Move!

Neutralizing is simply the process of not allowing conditions to be set up to your disadvantage. It is usually seen as yielding to a force, or an attempt to "grasp" or imbalance you, so that it counters the force with emptiness—you give them nothing to grasp. Neutralizing abates a relative condition that is not to your advantage. You simply prevent others from "inflicting" themselves upon you. It is integrally associated with being freely balanced (as mentioned earlier), since without neutralizing the forces that would disrupt your balance you would not be freely balanced for long in any interaction.

"A fly cannot alight"

If these principles are understood and actualized, I guarantee you will have greater functional ability in all that you do.

The power of Union and Inclusion
ON THE NATURE OF THE POWER OF INCLUSION

All powers are actually an appropriate balance of the two principal forces or principles of Union and Expansion. Any skill or ability depends on this balance. If we are conscious of this essential balance, the resultant power will be greater, and applicable to a wider variety of situations. Activities such as listening, engulfing, delivering force, taking a blow, uprooting, speed, being unmovable, using energy directly, affecting another with energy, balance, borrowing, joining, sticking and changeability are simply a matter of the balanced and appropriate use of the fundamental principles as they relate to the situation from moment to moment.

In Cheng Hsin all things should begin with a sense of connection, of not being separate from ourselves and others. To realize this state, we must allow our feeling-attention to flow out and into another or "external conditions," touching each completely. This corresponds to the principle of Expansion. At the same time, however, we must be receptive to their flow. We must let them in, and surrender to whatever arises. Also, we establish our own harmony of Being, consolidate our presence, and experience the moment. These correspond to the principle of Inclusion. We must do both in the very same instant, continuously! In this way we form a real union with others. From here it is possible to manifest all other powers, since the prerequisite, or true power, has already been established.

> See the 'statement' others are making. In any relationship, fighting, teaching or loving, get on the same side they are on, within their own directing and direction. Then your activity will align with theirs and your direction will be theirs; thus, they will then direct themselves in accord with you. First follow them, then join. Such is the case: destroying the hardness or violence is dilemma. Receive it, don't bang on it, accept it, then use it. View where they are coming from, see what they see.

Therefore, when I talk about the following Four Powers I am only speaking of distinctions in the same thing. Sometimes they are collectively called joining, sometimes following. With some investigation and consideration, you can notice that they are all, in fact, one event. I will only mention four, yet there are many more possibilities. If you penetrate to the heart of this principal distinction you will have access to all of the possibilities it represents.

FOUR POWERS

> *Let the opponent mold his own defeat as you are free to be molded.*

1. Following (Adherence)

> *Meet force with following (yield to it as it is).*

The fundamental method of following is continuously to follow and blend with whatever activity is arising. This course always insures that no excessive pressure is applied and, at the same time, that we do not disconnect from the activity. The secondary quality of adherence is constantly to seek the advantageous position through the feeling of relational positions. This is not done forcefully, but in harmony with our partner or situation in general. We can follow the very same movement into a detrimental position for ourselves or an advantageous one. Always choose the latter, maintaining a harmony with the activity and, at the same time, maintaining control over the situation without losing that harmony. As long as our actions are created within the context of following, we can do or create what we wish without contention with what is occurring. This basic method of following is the root of all of the powers of union. Quite simply, it is blending and following, without contention, staying in close proximity and active involvement with the activity around you. The fundamental principle involved in all of these distinctions is that our action is appropriately commensurate with what is occurring.

> *Adhere to activity and observe the requirements for an advantageous position.*

2. Contributing

Contributing arises out of following. While following, if an opponent takes forceful action designed to upset the balance of relationship with an act of his own, then "contribute" to that act, or "help him out," to further manifest the imbalance, and thus bring his action to a conclusion. However, in contributing we must remember that even though we are adding or giving our own energy to another's, this is still done with strict adherence to following. We must "help" the opponent, so to speak, and so join not only his movement but his intent as well. If he suddenly changes, we must change also, even while we are contributing to what has just taken place. So it is imperative to contribute or give energy only to the opponent's presently occurring action and intention; if it changes we have already changed. This works to the detriment of the opponent's position, and just exemplifies his tendency toward disharmony or imbalance created by his attack or manipulation of the situation.

Enter his rhythm and take control.

3. Borrowing

Borrowing is just that. We borrow the opponent's energy and movement and use it to move our own body as well as to attack his. We can borrow from touch, cycling his energy back to him, or catching his energy and springing it back on him; or borrow his intent and energy simply to move our own bodies. We can borrow energy without touch by allowing the opponent's intent and activity, apprehended via our listening ability, to direct our activity, adjusting to the changing circumstance, and so move us into appropriate actions.

Borrow his movement to adjust your own.

In borrowing we do not initiate or use energy of our own. We simply continue to use the opponent's energy, intention and movement to govern us, and so the opponent, by cycling and shifting and turning it back upon him.

4. Joining

Merge with him and, together, form a new direction.

Joining is frequently done without touching. It is most easily seen and studied, however, as the merging of two bodies and energies. In joining, we merge our activity with the opponent's activity, blending the bodies together and "joining in" on the motion that he (she) is creating, and so create a new one. This must be done so that it is not contrary to his motion, or against his motion, but redirects the energy so that he is helping us to destroy him in the moment of functional maturation. We must begin by completely accepting and following his energy and movement exactly the way they are. Then, as we merge, we begin to adjust the relationship so that we are both feeding a new purpose which happens to be to our advantage. In joining, we cannot be forceful, contrary, or protective of our established position. It is a very quiet and easy movement, and is not detected by the opponent until it is too late.

> *The above points actualized, result in communion or true union with others; simply Joining.*

Conclusion

The function of Cheng Hsin is inclusive of our whole life function. Although some of these points are more practically used in the context of martial function, most refer equally to all life activities, and the spirit behind all of the points is adaptable to everything we do. I am honored to be able to speak to you about them.

These functional considerations must eventually be brought into one state. Although while you train and practice you must investigate each distinction fully, you should also remember continually to bring the experience and discovery of what you learn into a sense of the whole. It is better to have a simple sense of one state of Being that is real to you than to have none as a result of not knowing which of these distinctions to choose simply because they appear to be different. Through training, work to bring this experience to a deeper, more powerful level. In the same way, develop your Cheng Hsin Body-Being. As you do you will begin to understand that this is the vehicle, and that the Cheng Hsin principles of function are the method of interaction which occur through this vehicle. They are indeed not different. The vehicle and its function exist for your transformation. Paradoxically, they need to be transformed as they are transforming.

Once the Cheng Hsin Body-Being and its functional condition are established as one state of Being, then nothing else need be done. All methods and advanced considerations or powers spring from this state, and are learned naturally and only to further the attainment of the highest levels of the art. Beyond this we must only look to further our complete adaptation to the true nature of Being.

Most honestly, I know of no other Way that is so inclusive, so far reaching, and yet so real and practical as this one!

Chapter Six

A Fundamental Consideration of Creating Ability

T he following considerations are presented as an opening into the question of being in relationship: specifically, respond- ing powerfully and generatively to what presents itself in relationship such that appropriate interactions arise—what we call skill or ability.

The principle of Inclusion

Know that the so-called 'solution' lies in the experience of the whole event, not within the contraction into the apparent prob- lem. This experience is inclusive and does not lie exclusively within or without.

The principle of inclusion is perhaps the most fundamental princi- ple in any consideration of ability. Indeed, it is the heart of ability. Inclusion should not be seen as one thing or be restricted to one dimension or concern. It is the inclusion of all that is occurring and every possibility of relationship on every level. Our first bar- rier to this principle usually arises in thinking its power lies in what we "know" about a situation or event. This is not so. Rather, its power lies in what we don't know, in the opening that is created in our encounter by including what's there without restricting it to how or what we think it is. Not that we deny what we think; thinking is included. We find however, that it is the opening, the embracing, the willingness to not-know that is the source of power in this principle of inclusion.

I want to present a few considerations that are consistent with this principle. As always, you must look into and through any individual viewpoint or consideration to grasp the actual principle at the foundation of these considerations.

CENTER INTELLIGENCE

This is an appropriate place to begin. Since our concerns always appear objectively, they can be related to a center. Even that which is not a body-related concern can be related to some notion of center; yet for our purposes, we will examine this phenomenon in the context of the psycho-physical.

Each of us is significantly defined by his or her existence as a thing or an object. As I've mentioned earlier, the Five Principles of Body-Being offer us the means to align ourselves with this condition; moreover, by positioning our awareness in the center region of the body we attain a capacity for relational understanding that is usually unexpected and overlooked. At first glance we may think that centering our awareness serves only body-movement ability. At second glance we see that a quality of calmness and a powerful attitude, or feeling positioning, arises as well. Yet we must look again, for an even more powerful alignment occurs.

That alignment permits us an experience that encompasses the myriad factors acting in relationship to produce the whole circumstance. In this process of inclusion—which thus brings everything into our field of experience—we gain access to the simultaneous relationship of every single body part and every possible combination of parts or factors, to every other part or combination of parts. If you consider this for a moment you'll see that the possible combinations of relationships are astounding, perhaps infinite, and in any case beyond mental comprehension. And we can encompass it all in one experience, merely by centering our attention.

Let me illustrate further. If from this position that is central to my whole body, I include in my experience everything that defines that position (the whole body), my experience then includes my right index finger as well as my left big toe. And what's even more fascinating, it also includes an instant comparison of the relationship the finger has to the toe at this moment: the distance between them, the direction of movement of each, an instant comparison of this movement, pressures occurring, and every other possible relationship that is occurring between them. Therefore, each influences the other in the whole experience to which they contribute. Now, if this is so for every other part of my body and every combination of parts (such as my feet, legs and pelvis in contrast to and in comparison with my hands, elbows and shoulders, or my left side with my right, or my back with my balance, and every other possible relationship), I have available a staggering amount of present experiential information. I instantly and continuously experience the relationships of my entire body (as long as my feeling-attention remains presently and openly located in the center and inclusive of the whole), and can make adjustments long before I can think out what those relationships are. However, the capacity we achieve does not end here.

Since each body part and sensation is related to every other part or sensation, any pressure or influence from external sources is immediately fed into this overall experience; and its relationship to any factor involved is determined or instantly included in our experience. Appropriate adjustments can thus be made spontaneously to all external influence. When we combine our visual and auditory perceptions with our body sensations, we have an instant comparative relationship with all that appears to comprise the event which is occurring. This is why it is so useful to allow ourselves to "feel" what we see or otherwise perceive. In this way we unify the whole experience, and instant relational comparisons are made across the board. It brings every objectified relational distinction into one balanced experience, as well as the relationship of each discrete element to every other.

What I'm calling "feeling" here seems to be the essential or "unifying" perceptive factor which more than likely constitutes our connection with what is called "life force." In any case, feeling certainly appears to be the generative event of movement or any volitional bodily activity, and by unifying our field of experience or perception in the domain of feeling, we gain an immediate and direct connection to and from bodily response or action. This is very important for any skill or ability that is determined by body movement. It appears that we have both a generative and a receiving relationship with this feeling-attention or "force of life." By establishing for ourselves the position of being that this consideration evokes, we have established a most sensitive and capable generative position from which to manage or create process.

Therefore, feeling-attention is held, deliberately and consciously, in the center part of the body. One area below the navel
in the abdomen is where attention, feeling, motivation and intuitive understanding are held or "put."

Since the center is at once the source of our movement and
unchanged by any movement or adjustment in relationship, it is
always complete. It exists completely in this moment, without
process and with nothing left out or left over. Its intelligence does
not linger in the past nor anticipate the future. Since it is the
center it is always free of any particular relationship; and yet is all
relationships, and unchanged no matter what the circumstance.
Conversely, it inherently encompasses every particular aspect of
every particle of this condition in this one moment down to the
nth degree. In the next moment it is *only* that moment and *free* of
that moment. It is now. It is complete. It does not move, yet *is*
movement.

*Nothing in this moment guarantees or means anything in the
next.*

Once we begin to open up to and accept the "intelligence"
that is found in aligning to this principle of center, we can begin
to adapt to the creative concerns that now may appear inclusive
and undivided, without leaving out any relational consideration,
no matter how complex or subtle. We should not be distracted by
the new capacity available to us. We must appreciate it, but when
we have become firmly rooted in it, we should move on to the
expansion that the rest of these points inspire.

USING THIS FEELING-ATTENTION

Whenever we move, stand or function in any way, it should be
done through a feeling-sense that we sometimes refer to as
"energy." It is not limited to the bounds or limits of the body.
When we speak of energy as a condition, it appears as an interactive factor that "is"; when we speak of energy as generated, this
is what appears as our feeling-attention, and can be shaped,
changed, or moved around. It is this "generative" energy distinction with which we are concerned here. When we speak of "using
energy," we are perhaps saying that the functional process that
we want to have occur is felt presently and totally before, during
and after its occurrence. This process is most effective when it is

engaged with sensitivity to the total condition in flux. The use of this "feeling-energy" brings into play every detail and all necessary considerations of function. Sensitivity to our body, its wholeness, its balance, and a feeling-direction of that whole, is using energy. Sensitivity to another's wholeness and to the relationship between the two, as well as feeling that and adjusting to that, is using energy. By placing our being in the position just described, we now have access to the generation of this particular state of "feeling-energy" and therefore can be in an appropriate and advantageous position with the whole, felt event.

When we want a particular functional result to occur, conceptualizing the condition or process necessary for the realization of that outcome, and then feeling and having that process "be," is a use of energy. Many times this goes beyond a present physical sense of what it would take to make a condition or a result occur. However, this process of conceptualization never strays from the present experience of that conceptual reality into mere abstraction. Rather than limit ourselves to an orientation of thinking about the mechanics of function—being held within the body and acting in relationship mechanically—we feel what the situation requires directly as an open possibility. We can then adjust our life force to the presence of any possibility, discerning what the feeling would be with or without the mechanics of the body, inclusive of them, but not limited to them. If we increase the use of energy and sensitivity, then we can decrease the use of mechanics and ordinary strength in order to achieve the same result.

The conscious direction of feeling-attention or energy, inclusive of a total body-feel and its relationship with everything, is the only way to include every facet and every level of functional relationship as it is occurring. Attempting to do something through the mind's direction of the mechanics can never accomplish the same results, since it is limited strictly to mental attention and our ability to direct all levels of mechanical movement. By letting all of our actions come from an inclusive feeling-sense, we make a quantum leap into a more effective realm of Being.

> *There is a state of being that shows itself as power, has free and uninhibited life force, with no thought or refuge being taken in the intellect, which honestly and simply abandons itself to the task at hand.*

There is also that which does not show itself and has nothing to grasp or notice, nothing to hide or show, and is so elusive in pursuit that, indeed, pursuit never even begins.

INTEGRITY OF BODY, LIFE FORCE AND CONCEPTUALIZATION

Simply put, when the entire attention is directly involved in the immediate direction of the body's movement, action or condition, through a feeling-awareness that encompasses the whole body and entire situation in this moment, then body, feeling, and awareness are not only in harmony but exist as one, and "mind" power becomes real. Conceptual direction then becomes powerful or objectively effective, since it is not separated from the present condition by thoughts about it, and so its very movement manifests as real. This is called intent.

When this state occurs in a physical sense, the three aspects (which are really distinctions in the same event) abide in the center of the body. The energy, mind and body not only merge, but arise from there. This should not be mistaken as a separation of their origin from their manifestation, for it simply represents, in a physical sense, a point of contact that all can relate to as the center or origin of appearance in the whole sense of Being. They are, however, completely inclusive of all conditions, since they are in fact one.

INCLUSIVE AWARENESS

Inclusive (engulfing) awareness is really a state of awareness or perception (including the feeling connection we call Life Force) brought about by an act of attention and openness. It is achieved when attention and feeling-awareness are freed to encompass all of the surroundings in present time, including any opponent, partner, or other relationship that may be occurring. This state generates a genuine feeling-sense of the whole environment, and empowers our responsiveness to it. We are then able to take a direct reading without intellectualizing. Another quality of this awareness is penetration, or "penetrating mind." I call it this because it entails a sense of penetration into objects, or another's body, energy and thinking, as well as the quality of engulfing them or including them.

Whenever you encounter anything and enter into relationship, begin always with the square peg as the square peg; the view as the view; the statement each individual is making, as is. After this, everything is taken care of naturally.

Inclusive awareness definitely applies to the primary relationship with which you are concerned, such as playing with a partner in front of you and engulfing his mind, body and energy. In this way you know what he is thinking. You feel his very body, breathing, and even his sweat! He has no thought that is not part of you. Everything he does is part of you. You are completely inclusive of him.

However, it must also be remembered that this inclusion does not restrict itself to that primary relationship. It must balance and be inclusive of the whole room or environment, and be equally inclusive all around, above and below. It also includes or engulfs every functional principle inherent in the design of this event, such as gravity, the earth, space, movement, timing, weight, balance, shape, appropriateness, and so on. The essential quality, however, is that the feeling-awareness fills out and includes or engulfs everything around you (including you), not trying to change it in any way, but completely accepting it as it is, continuously.

Adopting an 'engulfing' or 'inclusive' awareness is to surrender to the directness and realness of the event in this moment, and to merge with it in complete absorption and feeling-attention.

RECEPTIVE AWARENESS

A 'receptive attitude' is being open, with nothing to protect; allowing 'in' all aspects of this event in this moment.

Obviously, receptive awareness relates to inclusive awareness quite well, especially the "accepting-it-the-way-it-is" part. When we have a receptive attitude to that which we are including, it insures that we don't leave things out, or try to manipulate what appears with our concepts or feelings about "what" it is, or the "way" it is. Instead, we can let the situation be and feel it as it occurs or arises as an actual and present conditional reality. This includes feeling the physical, feeling the energy that is being used, and feeling the degree of consciousness that is involved. All levels, known and unknown, are included. By having a receptive attitude, we do not tend to recoil from what is there, but to relax in relationship to it. Therefore, we are better able to handle situations that arise, and change with them.

> *Yielding to the unyielding puts a demand on the ego not to cling that seems harder to fulfill the longer the demand persists. This requires an 'inner strength' to see beyond the apparent, and the patience to continue.*

CONTINUOUS LISTENING

> *It is only a lack of conscious awareness, experience in and from the source of the moment, that cramps appropriate changeability; and changeability is the demand of life, not holding a position or structure.*

Listening is an openness to feeling the condition of the world around and inside us. Most of the aforementioned points clearly require listening. It is in listening that we perceive and feel the energy flows, movement and intentions of others, and what is occurring in our own body-being.

Listening refers not only to the ability to sense a movement or an attack before it happens; it also includes knowing what is appropriate, sensing the right timing, and knowing when to wait. It applies to such things as knowing when it is time to conclude something, or when something needs more attention, more energy, or more time. Listening is appropriate to relationships other than psycho-physical interactions such as playing or fighting. It can also be used to ascertain the moods and intentions of people around us, how to relate to them, and even how we relate to knowing what or when to do something about or within our own self.

We can listen through touch, or without touch; through the eyes; and even on a sense-perception level without touch or sight. Each of these things should be transformed into a form that is "felt," and then all of them combined into one sophisticated feeling sense.

Listening is a very direct activity, and must remain directly connected no matter what the changing situation around us might be. When we are under pressure, we may correctly listen to and interpret movement, intention, energy flow, or timing; but then we get hooked onto that, or into meeting or responding to that action, and cease listening to whatever is arising behind, next or elsewhere. Thus, we do not notice a shift or change in the situation. For this reason, it is imperative to listen continuously. Not only is the situation or condition at hand listened to in this moment, but in the next, and the next, and the next. Even in the middle of activity involving what is actually occurring, we must continue to listen to that which is not yet manifest. This requires a real freedom and nonattachment, and a complete openness and willingness to change.

Dispassionate observation is involvement with no attachment to or fear of the outcome, and so lends great and continuous clarity.

Interpreting is essentially the second half of listening. Upon listening to or noticing something which is coming into existence, either as an intention or as a movement, we can spontaneously recognize it and know the various qualities it has, identifying it specifically. This is interpreting. In listening we often get a sense of the prior state of that which is coming into existence before it arises or develops any particular qualities—simply knowing on a level which precedes ordinary perception that something is arising. As we interpret that which is arising and notice its various qualities, we then know its "form." Thus we have at hand all the information necessary to interact with it. We know its timing, its direction, its intent, its power, its size, its length and any other relevant qualities. From this information we can create or respond appropriately.

As long as we are clearly and continually listening and interpreting, our actions will be appropriate. The moment that we forget to do this, however, our activity ceases to be in relationship to what is arising and begins to become our own "doing," or attempt to manipulate the situation; we fall out of grace with the real condition, and therefore will run into some problematic experience. This is why the creation of appropriate activity is ofttimes referred to as receiving. Although we are involved and responsive to a situation, we must also be completely receptive to it; in this moment, as it changes, and to any potential for change.

In a sense, listening is letting things be exactly the way they are, and interpreting is noticing that they are that way.

It is listening and interpreting that allow our actions to arise appropriately, and so determine the interaction and thus our skill or ability to interact. This is so because we are then directed by a sense of what is presently occurring; keeping the body-being aligned to natural functional principles, we can respond effectively.

Lending being

Do I turn the wheel or does the wheel turn me?

This point is as profound as its accomplishment is satisfying. It is the experience of realizing and surrendering to the truth that we, as individuals, are in fact only guests in life—guests of the principles and design that found us and allow for us to be. In what appears to be a commitment to our self or our own life and being, we find the access that we have to the "force" of being alive is exclusively devoted to the concerns of that self. This seems to us the only course for the purpose of serving self. However, this may not be so, and there are serious drawbacks to it.

In order to fulfill appropriately the demands of any given situation or event, whatever is occurring relationally as a whole must be dealt with, not just our side of the matter, and so our attention and concern must not be held exclusively to our self. This is where lending being comes in. "Being," or whatever it is that we seem to keep to ourselves, must be "lent" to or "given over" to whatever appropriately needs to "be" at any moment. This may appear as outside of us, within (or an aspect of) us, or something in between, something that appears as a function of *you* yet *not-you*, or as *not-you* but demanding *you* as a contributor for its beingness. Some examples of these:

> You: a feeling in your body.
> Not-you: someone else.
> In between: an interaction.
> A function of you yet not-you: the perception you have
> of another.
> Not-you demanding you: the effect you have on another.

These are only examples; the consideration should go much further than this. It is to any of these occurrences that we would "lend" being, which is to say we would lend the very force of life or being to them, to give what is usually held as exclusively ours to them such that they are empowered to "be." This is not a normal occurrence for us, or at least not noticed as such, and so appears irrational. The "how" is not important at this time; this is simply the consideration of the "lending."

> *Being with someone completely means to be open to them, and to our 'mind' (which for us is a survival function), this means revealing our whole self inclusive of that which we identify as good and bad. This is seen as a bad strategy to the protective activity called mind. It is not a bad strategy for being alive.*

We begin to notice that the experience of the situation of the moment does not lie inside or outside; it lies within the total event itself, and is beyond the activity of mind, or manipulation of our actions. Nevertheless, we persist in our efforts to control and manipulate conditions from an exclusive sense of self, and then wonder why we are not satisfied.

LENDING THE COMMITMENT OF SELF
TO THE WHOLE EVENT

Lending being, like being a guest, implies that we are not the "owner of the house" and are subject to the laws or ways of the household that we are visiting. Since no individual or thing is the master of this "house," each is subject to the same law. A primary expression of alignment to this law is balance and equilibrium; we must adjust and be subject to the natural flows and demands of energy and life. If another acts contrary to the "balance of things" or "breaks the law," he will be returned to it as a matter of course. We simply remain in harmony with, arising from and surrendering to, the source that *is* the master of this house, and may or may not be an instrument in his return.

Even our center intelligence surrenders to the Intelligence that is the source of this condition and of being alive The ability to accomplish this is closely linked to our ability, or willingness, to relax or let go.

This is simply relaxing the sense of control to forces, already in operation, which are not knowable in the usual sense—nor are these forces attainable or controllable in, and as, an individual who maintains a sense of separation from them, which is the sense of being a self exclusively.

"I" is a sense of identification as a structure that is separate from, and endangered by, structures that are not it. We must remember that relaxing this commitment (to the exclusive pursuit and being of I) does not have to "look" a particular way. It must relax, however.

We often think that ego means arrogance, pridefulness, self-centeredness. We thus believe that someone who is apparently weak, humble, fearful, or quiet has less ego than one who is apparently flamboyant, strong, opinionated or fearless. This is not so. The form has nothing to do with it. The "flamboyant" personality can have less attachment to its ego-structure than the apparently "reserved" personality. The shy person has as much "ego" as the apparently fearless person. The forceful personality often feels as endangered by the world as the cowering one. Regardless of type, character, or personality, it is all the same event.

So, when I say relax the commitment to self, I simply mean to relax the identification or attachment to maintaining your particular structure, appearance, and desire to "win." Relax the fear of losing and the sense of separateness. What occurs at this point is a feeling of openness, presence, and being with whatever happens, unconcerned with any result, simply aware and open to this moment in time.

To be sure, this does not mean to be uninvolved, withdrawn or indolent. If the situation demands a high level of energy and action, then that will naturally occur. We simply have no binding attachment to the outcome.

Our structure of disconnection is held strongly in place by our attitudes, beliefs and fears. We therefore relax structural limits by relaxing that which holds them in place. Many of these are so deeply ingrained that we don't even know they exist. Even with our first investigations, they do not show themselves. This is another reason why we should not attempt to "appear" like anything in particular to accomplish this, since we are not cognizant of many of the fundamental structures that are involved. Further, that is why this is a training, and requires "ability."

To a greater or lesser degree, when we relax our hold on what seems to us to be the necessary restrictions to the body-self and its protection, we feel a sense of surrender to something. In this case, it can simply be surrendering the walls of our attitudinal confines to fall into the greater structure of the whole. When that occurs, our life force then fills out and becomes a part of our surroundings.

By letting go of our exclusive commitment to self, we reach a position of openness, of pure Being, where we are able to receive, "read" and respond to life demands as they arise.

LENDING BEING COMPLETELY

When you are involved in anything, notice how quite frequently not all of you is involved. When you are overly involved and focused on a result in a future moment, then you are not totally in this one. If you hold something back or in reserve, have thoughts that are not about what is happening now, or at least not supportive of the present experience and activity, then you will be divided and not total.

When you enter into the absolute presence and fill out your life force and feeling-awareness on all sides, you are total and unified. From this totality and integrity you can then give the whole self or life force to whatever is appropriate, and not hold back or be divided by apparently conflicting commitments.

Giving being

To present the distinction of giving being comprehensively is somewhat beyond the scope of this work. However, I want to create an opening that goes beyond the possibilities represented thus far in this consideration. Giving being is a lot like lending being. It entails bringing something into being, into the presently-occurring event, creating something that would otherwise not "be." Therefore, this consideration must stand on and include everything mentioned in "The Principle of Inclusion" and "Lending Being."

NON-ACTION

To set the stage for further discussion of giving being, I want to address the principle of non-action. In this case, objective descriptions are wholly insufficient, for non-action can be grasped only through the experience. For our purposes, however, I will touch upon some of the concepts that tend to arise out of such an experience.

I will describe one of the times when the significance of non-action became apparent to me. The story sounds like a typical tale of its kind, full of mountains and water and nature; nevertheless, those manifestations were simply the circumstances of its occurrence, not to be confused with anything "natural" versus "unnatural."

During a period of intense personal study, I was staying at the mountain camp of one of my friends, observing things around me and hanging out by myself a great deal. While sitting on a rock by a stream, observing the movement of the water down through the rocks, it occurred to me that at any point the water was the same; to any particle of water, the journey did not exist as movement from one point to another. It simply was what it always was—not experiencing the slightest exertion, and actually doing nothing. I was struck by the fact that there were places where the water fell rapidly, stretches where it was silent, places where it had to move quickly around a rock, sections where it was effervescent, and places where it was pooled. Throughout this variety of activity the water was exactly the same, and all of those "conditions" as a whole were being met exactly, with no confusion, and no effort. In the same moment, the same water was effervescent and silent, calm and falling, moving and still, and perhaps a dozen other qualities as well.

I realized that this represented a principle that would be valuable for body-being adaptation: that our own body has to be transfigured in such a way, and our own feeling-attention has to dwell in a consciousness that can meet countless varieties of circumstance all at the same time and without disturbance.

Some time later, I was sitting in a field just observing the movement of trees and wind, grass and earth, and it was then that I had the experience of non-action. I realized that, in fact, nothing is really occurring. No plant, animal, or element is "doing" anything. The change in space is totally relative.

For example, as the water moves along and then falls down in a waterfall it does nothing. If the water fell up, then it would be doing something! As a tree grows it does nothing. It simply fills the space and function that is demanded of it, given that life and being manifests as it does; and if existence changed, and manifested in some other way, then that would be the nature of things. And still nothing would be occurring. If the tree "grabbed" itself and did not grow, then it would be doing something.

The only event that seemed contrary to this was being human.

Man apparently does things. In truth, however, even man has absolutely no choice about what he does. Only the way in which he perceives his actions and the directness with which they are accomplished does not adhere. Therefore, the resistance to the truth that nothing is really going on separates us from non-action. In a sense, we can make this practical by experiencing the constancy of equilibrium behind all that occurs. In this and every moment, we thus create access to the realization of the immediate course that would be followed naturally if our distorted sense of consciousness did not interfere. This principle is aligned to the source of Being called Cheng Hsin.

One functional application this understanding produces is an ability to adhere effortlessly to *dispassionate observation* with our feeling-attention. Dispassionate observation is simply an unperturbed mind and attention that is non-reactive, non-judgmental and continually present. Not only must our awareness adhere, but the body state itself, and the function of the body. Every action continues to relate to balance and equilibrium in the principle of non-action. Thus, our actions follow "design," fulfilling the energy that is being directed by the situation and the relationship, and therefore our actions are not "doing" anything. Even the force we use adheres to non-action, for it springs from gravity and relaxation.

> *Our actions are not our own*
> *but follow the Way of the environment.*
> *We do not try,*
> *but step here*
> *or there*
> *and allow the outcome to occur.*

GIVING BEING

Non-action creates a platform of emptiness from which to "hear" and consider the distinction of giving being. Giving being does not appear to arise from us as a self, or from anywhere else; it seems to be both received from "reality" and given or made real by one's self. It is necessary to have some "nothing" with which to consider a distinction that can only be thought of as irrational, unthinkable or existential.

Giving being is not an exclusive function. It does not arise from the whim of a self. Conversely, it seems only to arise from one's intent and participation. It *is* the bringing of something into being, and yet we are not speaking of bringing any "thing" or object into being. Rather, we bring a quality or state into being, or an alignment to a principle, an activity, a relational condition, a perception, ability, a force or power, a process, no process at all, a skill, interpretation, knowingness, sensitivity, or anything else that is appropriate to the event of being as it appears. When I say appropriate, I don't mean that it is logical or that it naturally follows from what appears to be. As a matter of fact, giving being appears as not arising out of circumstance. It is not a result or effect of what appears as the condition or history of this moment. However, such an occasion must be completely inclusive of all that appears to be.

Since we already give *being* to the perception of what *is* (in other words, we acknowledge its "beingness"), and to interpretation itself, it is necessary to move our cognition-attention and life force to a position of Being in which this can be recognized as already and actually the case. We can then give being to what is not at present occurring.

This can not be done in conflict with anything, since anything with which it would be conflicting has already been interpreted by us, and this conflict would displace the appearance or beingness of that which is not. We would be in conflict with our own interpretation. When we align to the source of that which is already giving being to what is, we are not in conflict. Conflict is usually a function of the exclusive desire to change what appears to be. Giving being, however, occurs only when it *is* what appears to be. Since that which appears to be continuously changes, that which is *given being* arises or becomes what appears to be.

Giving being is not personal in any way. It is creating an opening in which something that is not now being or being interpreted as here, or as "real," can take on "beingness," and be interpreted as present. We may conceptualize the possibility of something and still not call it real or really happening, because it does not appear as received from not-us as well as interpreted by us. Therefore, we must both receive it, as if not of our own making, and give it, as if willed into being by us, for it to become real or appear as effective in our interactions with things and others.

Chapter Seven

Cheng Hsin Applied to an Art Form

PART ONE: THE PRACTICE OF AN ART

The value of form is obtained by understanding the correct relationship to and purpose of form. We must see the nature of limits (form) first. Form arises from formlessness; the first requirement for creating a limit is that there is none.

Practicing an art is studying one's own event, which appears for us as our experience, expression and relationships—or life itself. Art, meditation, love, human expression, spirituality, integrity, zen, honesty, excellence, essence, may all be words about the same thing. Although the "form" of things may not change, such a practice constitutes the difference between surviving in suffering and living in joy.

A FORM OF PRACTICE

Often what is said in this chapter is applicable to a wide variety of arts and endeavors. These considerations, however, are grounded in the study of internal martial art; not necessarily in the "tradition" or beliefs of some system or other, but in the free investigation of the mechanics, dynamics, and principles that seem to comprise psychophysical interaction, specifically as it relates to the mechanics of an effortlessly powerful body-being and to the art and craft of fighting.

When applied to an art form, the study and practice of Cheng Hsin can be effectivley done in the context of the internal martial arts, or the practice of psycho-physical interaction such as is found in the art of fighting interaction. Arts such as T'ai Chi Ch'uan, Hsing I-Pa Kua, swordplay, boxing and Aikido lend themselves well to a complete study of the many dimensions and aspects of Being that found our experience. This is why I use these arts as the tool with which to teach and study Cheng Hsin, the nature and dynamic of Being. (Also, because they're fun.)

We must remember, however, that whatever "idea" we form of Cheng Hsin is not Cheng Hsin, even if is a quality that arises in, as, or from it. An idea or concept of Cheng Hsin is limited; that is the nature of conceptualization. Cheng Hsin itself, however, is the Absolute nature of Being. Therefore, it is also T'ai Chi, the undifferentiated-absolute. Any idea sets itself apart from other ideas, thus it cannot be undifferentiated; as a concept, it cannot be absolute.

If this sounds extreme, remember that understanding this sort of thing is an extreme and uncompromising affair; however, I have an even more practical reason for such a presentation. It is very conducive to our development to realize that whatever concept we have of our condition, and of our understanding of what we do, it is not complete, and therefore not actually correct. We maintain a constant condition of limitation; our aim is not to fight that condition, but continually to realize it. In this way, we are frequently, if not constantly, able to transform our approach and our ideas about what we do and how we are.

Therefore, as we undertake such a study, it is useful to understand that our purpose is not to add something else to our individual structure or limited sense of self, but to open that up and to realize the fundamental nature of our existence as it is. So we strive to "turn into," to feel, to intuit, to realize what is so, having stripped away the sense of separation from that—and this is not done by adding more complications in limitation. This process is sometimes challenging and sometimes threatening to our ego, but its underlying qualities can be those of simplicity and enjoyment.

About your relationship to practice

The principles of Cheng Hsin, expounded briefly in this book, are the functional requisites and foundation for practicing any Cheng Hsin art. Consider this.

You probably have some idea that studies such as T'ai Chi and

Aikido deal with changing the body, freeing the mind, and developing the energy or life force. Although development of the energy inherent to the body-being and mind is of primary importance, it is not the purpose. It is rather a preparation *within* "Cheng Hsin" to realize "Cheng Hsin." This process, inclusive of bodily transformation, is itself the creation of a vehicle and tool for the function of an art. Even this function is not the end but the ground in which understanding may take place.

Without the development of the functional aspects of these arts, a real understanding and development of energy and awareness cannot be attained, nor will the ultimate aim of our practice be properly realized. Practicing the technique alone, in the form of sets of movements or routines for development, may lead to an increase in health, provide exercise, and develop the feeling-awareness, but it will fall far short of the level of functional development these routines were originally designed to train. Through this study of movement and relationship we may observe and adhere to a natural process. It is through the "play" of these arts that we learn to establish an understanding of continuity throughout interaction, within which we may realize and manifest the principles.

When I speak of Cheng Hsin as a study or art, I'm referring to a natural process which has only one source, but does not adhere to any particular method of revealing that source. When we greet someone, we choose a particular way to greet him which reveals the source of the greeting that has no form.

Nevertheless, we must, at least for convenience, choose a form or structure in which to interact. Yet I also want to communicate the source of techniques, and the way of "what is." As Musashi said:

> *The principle of the way of strategy is to have one thing to know ten thousand things.*

Cheng Hsin appears to be obscure and complex at first glance. It seems to embrace indirectness; however, the heart of Cheng Hsin is quite simple and extremely direct. We habitually see and engage in superficial or simplistic relational realities in the world. Thus, directness has often come to be equated with bluntness and grossness. In Cheng Hsin, however, we look to establish a more supreme directness, one that touches Being and embraces paradox. The obvious is not always seen as such, since our minds deal so often in excessive complications.

Some form of body-being practice

Naturally, it is the posture of the body-being, and the movement of changing from one posture to another, that begins and remains the study of any art of movement. However, once the body's movement begins to conform properly, then energy development must become the focal point and real function of the movement.

Let's review some important things to remember throughout this kind of practice. To begin with, we must place our weight into the feet, not just on them; and our feet into the ground, not merely on it. With the body balanced and resting in the feet we begin movement. The energy lifting any part of the body (the hands, knees, feet, et al.) comes from a deliberate sinking or draining of tissues and feeling-attention down into the foot and earth. As this movement goes down, the object being lifted is raised as if connected to a pulley that is attached to the sinking. Thus, all parts are earthbound, rising with an absolute minimum amount of force. At any time, anything—muscle, bone, a finger, wrist, toes, whatever—that is not actively moving for a functional purpose simply remains relaxed and follows the movement of the whole. Remember that this is a never-ending process as things go through a cycle of being used minimally and end by falling relaxed completely. Multiples of tissues are constantly at various stages of this process and a myriad of body parts are involved in different ways. One part may be letting go as another begins activity, but they all work together. Therefore, the process that is felt is one of overall and continuous relaxation.

Next, the whole body-being must move in unison and in total. In the beginning a lot of attention should be put on the pelvis; all movement should be designed to emanate literally from the pelvis and center. If you do not feel this or understand it in some move, investigate it radically until you do. Once the direction of all parts from the center has been established, you can begin the important unification and filling out of the whole and total energy in and around a relaxed body.

All of the points established in the earlier chapters should be taken and incorporated into your routines. They are not to be freely rendered or adapted through your imagination or interpretation. They should be understood, not molded into a form you can accept. You may not grasp their importance immediately. If grasped, excitedly at first, enjoy them and grow with them to be sure, yet remain open to what they will continue to teach you if your perseverance and dedication to investigation is true. It is simple but real, and therefore personal honesty is a factor.

Moving posture

Posture is by no means stagnant. The principles of posture must be followed throughout our movements. Just as a piece of clay is still clay no matter what shape it takes, we must continually apply the principles. All forms and actions are nothing more than moving posture, so it is important to move properly in order to align to the principles of body-being. Stay relaxed, balanced, and comfortable, and use the body as one unit; with this alignment our actions will be easy.

When we take a step and then shift our weight, the stepping foot should set the distance, and relax into the spot where it is placed. Do not hold it off the ground; let the whole leg and at least some of the weight go into it. As this occurs, the pelvis relaxes towards that direction, and the whole body (upper resting on lower) moves in that direction. This occurs at the same time and as a function of sinking into the other foot and leg. The whole body is involved in this relaxing and pressing of the weighted foot squarely into the ground. So, as that leg is being filled, the weight starts to move forward as well as down. Generally, when we are standing still in a posture we keep most of the weight either in the back foot or the front (usually 60–70%). To shift the weight, the weighted leg then lets go or collapses, following the movement of the body as it moves toward the foot that stepped. As the weight dips toward the ground it presses into the newly-weighted foot and is established there. The procedure is the same for moving forwards or backwards. The distance between the feet is not important; that movement occur naturally and correctly is essential.

Aligning with the principles

The fundamental training of the body-being lies in the use of feeling or "energy." Whether flowing in specific channels, or adopting a state (or functional conceptual condition), the feeling-energy is primary. Training the body mechanics to adapt to sound physical principles is the first step, but this can only be done if body-feel and its direction enters into study, and this brings energy into play.

Feeling is primary in using energy. As you stand, move or make changes, continue to increase your ability to feel what you are doing as a whole: mentally, emotionally, what you feel inside, outside, and underneath you. As the mechanics become more and more finely adjusted, you may begin to feel movements in energy that seem to have little to do with your direction of them. Simply notice what is the case, with yourself and with the way things are.

Of course, feeling the mechanics and persisting in their training is a must. This is your art. Make it yours by becoming at home with its movements, so that they come about naturally and spontaneously through your appropriate expression in changing conditions.

While practicing sets of movements or techniques, concentrate on the wholeness in your expression, as well as its relationship to space, earth, and/or another. At first you must establish your own center as master over the extremities, by changing the body's habit of moving as separate parts to moving as one whole directed from the center. Next, establish that the feeling-energy all passes through and relates to that center, and let your attention reside there.

We are then ready to establish a powerful relationship with space (three-dimensions), and with the earth (grounding). Imagine that the legs slip into something much larger and more equally distributed than themselves (like the water drop), with some feeling of thickness that fills the space in between and all around them. By also "plugging" into the earth's massive depth through the bottom of the feet, we draw our power and motivation to the center. Never leaving this "plugged-into" state, we can channel and direct the energy through the center and out the arms (or wherever) and relate to the space around us.

Feeling and playing in the entire space that surrounds the body is very important. Learn to fill out and circulate the feeling throughout the body, and to extend it out past the hands or radiate from the whole body all at once. Keep a balance of awareness on all sides. Whenever we focus a lot of energy outward (energy extension), that flow should be balanced by centering and grounding our feeling-attention.

As we begin to relate all of this to an interaction with other people, we must find the center of the relationship and relate to that. The feeling-energy must now blend with theirs and follow them to a natural breaking point created by their use of energy and intent, whether it's done consciously on their part or not.

The essence of routine training lies in obtaining body-being mastery and expressing the life force through it. Body-feel is a must, as is the training and stretching of the tissues, so that you can create a full and dynamic expression of energy in an art form. It is getting to know yourself through your relationship with body movement, and through the process of developing a free expression.

The study of a set of movements is a study of your relationship to your body, your history, your person, your limits, the ground, and your immediate environment. Make no mistake; it is a study of your very existence as a bodily being. It is an opportunity to bring into being an integrity of body, movement, and function.

Functional theory

The obvious beginning of functional theory in these interactive arts lies in the concept of **yielding**. But yielding is not done alone, as exhaling is not done alone; it must be complemented by **following** or **sticking**. Four ounces (the weight of one cube of butter) is the usual measure of pressure we apply when contacting another mass. In yielding we usually allow no more than four ounces to alight on the body. In sticking we allow no less than four ounces to leave the body. If we look at the constancy of that pressure it becomes more apparent that sticking and yielding are just relative adjustments, depending on the point of view, to accomplish the same thing. Therefore, the old T'ai Chi Classics say: "To stick is to yield, and to yield is to stick." We must yield to follow an opponent's withdrawal, as we must stick to his aggressive action; they cannot be separated and still be effectively done.

We want to let the opponent move us and not withdraw ourselves, and so avoid expending energy, disconnecting, or losing sensitivity to the balance between exact pressures and subtle shifts in direction and intention. Although some part may be attacked that weighs more than four ounces, still no more than four ounces alight, because the whole body is relaxed and adjusts with flexibility in all of the joints (being loose and free), and the weight is drained from that area to compliment the force and still comply with adherence.

So, it becomes apparent that the essential activity and principle that we are addressing is that of *following*—to "give up yourself and follow the opponent." Remember, in order to find the appropriate action or response at a touch, the body should be like water, the mind empty and open, so that:

> *The opponent molds his own defeat by his very actions as you are free to be molded.*

Interactive practices

Interactive practices and techniques, although structured, should be formed in such a way as to reveal a way of change. It is in these practices that you get a feel for the active use and function of the movements. You can also develop an understanding of the method of continuous change and practice relaxing and following the principles and posture points under a more demanding and active set of circumstances.

The idea is constantly to change so that your action renders the opponent's immediate or impending action useless, and to attack the weakness or opening that he has created by his action. But since at any time he can change and attack again, your action must also be conducive to a continuance, and change into whatever the next appropriate action might be. You are then being with what is, and in tune with what is becoming; in this way you maintain a continuously-changing, appropriate activity. Remember that your action is entirely subject to the opponent! As your own action is being overcome, it changes into an action that overcomes that which is overcoming.

Footwork

Because my communication of footwork is more of an understanding of possibilities in spatial geometry than it is a particular form of study, most students neglect its importance and fail to do it justice. I have had no student seriously study footwork fully, so that they even approach me in understanding or ability in this respect. I can only teach it so far, point the way, so to speak. Then it is the responsibility of the serious student to dwell, consider, and study. With practice, contemplation, study, and inquiry, the student is free to open the door and enter; without them, he will not even see the door!

This is an art of movement, subtle and gross. As I once defined it: "Stepping is basically an adjustment of the waist and legs to accommodate a force." Contemplate that statement, and how it relates to all that you do in your art.

People usually think that the objective of anything is to "know" it, meaning to learn of it or its appearance. This kind of knowledge doesn't do any good in developing skill. Knowing is like a tool: it serves no purpose unless used, and to use it you must know more than just of its existence and shape! You must know its meaning, its skill, its function; and it must be available to you through practice and understanding.

Stepping is not only agility; it is strategy. I wish to quote from several sections in private manuals. The following refers to my basic footwork patterns:

> The feet can form many geometric patterns. The basic patterns cover the bulk of necessary stepping when mixed freely in combat. Of course, they are mostly to develop agility in moving the weight and positioning the body through the adjustment of the waist and legs, and for you to become familiar with various patterns of movement. It requires a lot of spontaneous ingenuity and imagination to interchange, reverse, make big or small, and mix them up as required by the situation, to create infinite patterns of possibilities. When in actual engagement the best way to follow is to relax the legs in a loose, sunk, and rubbery manner, so that they answer to the dictates of force and influence, and fall naturally where the situation demands!

To become skillful at stepping you must release clinging; leave any space; attach yourself to no idea, form or place. Simply let it go, but have control by letting it be. Maintain a relaxed and natural posture as you move, and open your pelvis. All of the points mentioned in every prior page apply. Allow the light foot continually to reestablish contact with the earth; don't hold it up. Similarly, let the whole body follow the center at its slightest stir.

Before you can move anywhere you must sink straight down into the foot on which you are standing. You could push off of it, but this will eventually get you into trouble. It is relaxing and falling away that allows you not to cling. Continuous change happens by giving up, not by pushing and demanding.

Regarding boxing skill:

> When adjusting your steps, not only must they be pleat-like, they can be ordered to limit his ability. For example, when you find yourself, for one reason or another, evading more than attacking, step to make his blows more singular. Make it difficult, by the directions you move, for him to follow up and be multiple. This will allow you to regain your advantage.

The "boxing" arts

When practicing boxing, the limbs should remain constantly relaxed. When you want to move quickly, for power or for evasion or both, sink (press) the one foot. By dropping your weight and feeling-attention into one foot, you can then gather that force into your pelvis to move the center quickly, and so direct your whole body's movement. Sacrum-pelvis must connect with heel-sole. This will provide you with a method of evasion that will allow you to move out quickly, in one piece. When striking, it delivers intrinsic strength (force) from the earth. Often you will need to do both at the same time. Such is the case in the following example: Pressing one foot, and remaining in balance, rotate the pelvis to turn one side of the body away from an attack, or perhaps tilt it as in a dodge; this creates evasion. Finding an appropriate step, you then transfer the weight by relaxing that leg (the hands are simply following the body all the while) and pressing what is now the newly-established weighted foot; this act creates the blow. This happens in one motion, but remember to press first one foot, then the other; failure to do so will greatly reduce your ability, speed, and power. The same principle applies to all movements in boxing.

In the boxing arts, many circumstances demand complete control and speedy movement of the center to accomplish an evasion. To move the whole body as fast as someone can move his hand requires that you become adept at pressing your foot, and quickly and efficiently using that power suddenly to launch or turn your waist. You must move your center and turn your pelvis as fast as your opponent can punch.

Wu Tsan Ch'un (Misty-Body Boxing)

I created Misty-Body Boxing as a practice for developing many useful and needed fighting skills. It is the constant endeavor in Wu Tsan Ch'un to follow the opponent completely, continuously hitting him with the softest blows, but without letting him put one ounce of pressure on you! The objective is to move totally in accord with the opponent, never resisting or blocking in any way, nor allowing any blows to touch you. Your hands and feet always touch him lightly; whether evading or attacking, you use no force. Your body is as a mist to him; he cannot get any substantial grasp of it, nor can he keep it out.

Follow his every move, his every thought! You now need all the coordination and integration you have gained by doing your body training correctly, and all the fine distinctions, balance, skill and relaxedness you've developed. The routine double practices and techniques become useful, free, and formless. You should see how all that you've done begins to come together, how it relates and is necessary. You will also find that mastery of the Principles of Cheng Hsin is essential. If you have studied, practiced, and understood, then it will serve you greatly. If not, you will not be able to do what is required of you, and will be forced to go back to the foundation and study until it becomes a part of you.

We must also have a method with which to study intrinsic strength and its natural application and use for power. I use the art of Cheng Hsin T'ui Shou and boxing (with gloves) to serve this function. The study of all that is required for functional ability is necessary before one can become adept at an advanced level. This is preparation for a study such as Huan Sheng, which is my advanced interactive art (and so addresses metaphysics as well as ontology).

The animals and mind

Many famous martial arts derive at least some of their conceptual framework from a study of animals. Several histories of warriors tell of watching animals fight or adopting something from some animal or other. But what was really seen; what was the inspiration? Was it just from seeing the form of the animals fight?

I am going to quote from something I wrote many years ago, after having a realization on this subject during a tour of Asia in 1975. It was my habit to visit zoos at every place I went and this consideration was the result.

> . . . The feeling-attention plays a much larger role, for Tu (the energy that creates harm) is not expressed without it, and power is not let loose without the freedom to express. The use of all these skills however, is not possible if their manifestation isn't appropriate and spontaneous. Fear destroys this ability, and creates a lack of the mental clarity and direction necessary to allow the physical ability to come about.
>
> The physical body must succumb to the energy or feeling, which is directed (instantly and in any form) by consciousness (not to be confused with reason). The relaxed physical body can manifest in movement subject to change and external influence, because it has no 'mind of its own.' Power must be channeled throughout the whole body, which must adopt the proper functional alignments, and this can only be done if the feeling-attention consciously follows the appropriate paths. The fight, however, is a relationship, and 'to know yourself and your opponent' requires much more than physical energy or even skill. Here, animals are clearly worth studying.
>
> Many animals show a distinct and clear inner strength and spirit—not of an egoic or a self-conscious nature, but a clear and strong force of being—which allows tremendous physical tenacity. I'm sure the originators of the arts based on animals were as interested in the minds and spirits of these animals as they were in the physical aspects. These animals show exceedingly strong inner will and clarity, with no ego-fear (as we know it) to block tenacity; and no confusion due to reason's failure to control the world. Also, they have no concept of themselves or their manifestation that is not true, accurate, and to-the-point. No separation in thought-of-themselves and what they are! Nothing hidden.
>
> To know yourself you must be conscious of your own weakness; then it is no longer a weakness, for it is only mind and cannot be destroyed! If you present it fully to your opponent it becomes a particular form of 'inner' strength. If it is not hidden, it will not turn into fear. However, it is frightening to another to see someone present his weakness (fear) outright; and because you are conscious of what it is, you need not fight its existence or appearance. This allows you to stand open and

free of confusion or doubt, and experience your very presence—and this is power!

To know your opponent is to 'see' this weakness and deepest fear. To see through to what he wants to keep hidden from the world and himself is to destroy him before the fight begins!

To 'make the hair stand on your body like a cat' is not to tense or lose control, but to allow the dynamic energy of the situation to be felt and channeled up your spine and through your body. A tiger has such clarity and bearing when facing an enemy because he knows only 'tiger' energy and has no self-consciousness or doubt, and will meet the situation without confusion. What we see in the directness and power of animals comes from their very Being. This openness and directness of Being that is created by having nothing hidden and little ego is worth studying and adopting.

PART TWO: WHAT DOES FIGHTING HAVE TO DO WITH CONSCIOUSNESS?
SOME POINTS ON THE ART OF FIGHTING
Practical understanding—in relationship to abilities

In order to be effective in any relational art you must always know the intent and strategy of the others involved. Wait unceasingly for their intentions and impulses. Equally important is to know yourself, to be clear about your purpose and objectives for the interaction, never making your purpose servant to the strategy of the moment. Keep an inclusive awareness; have no gaps; link consciously all parts of your being. Develop a willingness to experience (no fear), taking responsibility for the entire interaction (which is simply full participation in the demands of life).

Develop the ability to "see" the opponent's framework, and use it to create a relationship to that event in this moment that allows you to see him as harmless; to create a context for action that can handle whatever course he may take. Thus by a simple act of observation you can recognize his activity as manageable and as potential, and relate to each in his own way. "See" the opponent (penetrate his mind and context). This allows the time and space to create, prior to his actions, your own complimentary actions.

In every event that arises as a process, we observe a sequence to the changes. The beginning sees a birth, which turns into growth, then maturity, and finally completion or dissolution. All process must arise in this way. If we adhere to this understanding and use it, we can establish an appropriate relationship to every changing moment of the process or event. Without preparation, the beginning will not be appropriately engaged. Certain things must be done at the right time in order to be effective. For example, if I commit myself to a response at the "growth" stage, in expectation of an extrapolated course of action, the opponent is free to recognize and change his action, and I will become inappropriate to the event. On the other hand, at this very same stage it is easier to alter the course of impending process. At the "maturity" stage, when the process is accomplishing its task, alteration is most difficult. Yet since this is true for both sides, his ability to adjust his action to accommodate an attack of mine timed to appear at this stage will be severely hampered. At completion, most people don't have a full appreciation of the remaining effects of the passing process. They are restricted from moving freely into the next moment of new process; their balance and momentum is trapped and they are defeated by their own inability to respond.

Realize that both creating and destroying are the same, and so exist in the same event. Only point of view separates them; to know this allows us to remain appropriate to what needs to be let go of in our activity or handled in the activity of the opponents, as well as what needs to arise or can arise. Then we can change appropriately, allowing the changes to act as one process. With this base of understanding we can complement and make inappropriate (destroy the function of) his actions, as well as give rise to the next appropriate movement, blending both into one activity.

Learning from the animal's mind—which appears as extremely direct, open, and free from pretense—we see and can adopt a position of being that seems to produce a strong life-force with a clarity of intention, fullness of vitality, and an overwhelming bearing. We are thus empowered with the ability and impulse to keep nothing hidden. This in turn allows us the clarity necessary to penetrate what the opponent wants to keep hidden, which always appears to himself as weakness, badness, fear, or incapacity (the operating principle of which is found in the mind's judgement-protection syndrome). This understanding contributes to one of our primary goals in the art and training of fighting: not to separate or differentiate the thought or concept of our self from what we are actually manifesting in the event.

In interaction, all of the points, principles, and "mechanics" that have been discussed serve only to achieve **following**, upon which all abilities depend. It is union, transcending the separation of one's activity from another's activity. **Non-interference** is a key to complementing and joining. In "action" maintain non-interference; do not even interfere with yourself. The key is what you do not do. The essence of this lies in the mind. Our tendency is to commit to and entrap our action in an ego-fulfilling expression. In every moment we extrapolate conceptually the future of the present condition; we then adopt a position of "knowing what to do," either as an impulse to react or as an expression that serves our image or accomplishment. In this our force is dedicated to fulfilling a particular course and so breaks off open and plastic relationship with the next moment of activity. In so doing we have interfered with the joining or appropriate interaction from moment to moment, and are no longer "following." When this principle is broken we become only randomly effective.

To join another for the purpose of managing his force and action, you need to join his "feeling-attention," so to speak. Trying to affect the physical alone is inadequate to our task. You need to have an effect on his action by affecting the energy which governs it. As a Chinese boxer once said: "As soon as I have touched his clothes he is immediately thrown over." Merge all of you with all of him (mind, body, energy, movement). If he attacks in some fashion he must be in range, so you can "join" him. Keep him stuck to your body; wherever he touches, yield and stick to that part. Adapt to changes. Throw or join as he tries this or that, and turn his force back onto him in a circle; let him end with his own beginning.

Fill space and leave space in complement. The timing of this must be no sooner than will allow for his commitment, nor later than his involvement. He receives force or impact when he feels it is the moment for his own force or impact to occur.

In order to throw someone away without using great strength or a lot of pressure, you can accelerate, contributing to his movement or stillness, at a constant pressure and create a multiple effect. Thus without adding more than a few ounces you can achieve what many pounds would have achieved if applied all at once.

When receiving force from any source, remain calm and sunk. In this way you can neutralize, absorb, or join that force without losing balance or being adversely affected by it. This is also true when taking blows.

The art of evasion

The art of evasion demands the coordination of many activities in an apparently simple event and small space of time. You must determine the "kind" of action that you are to evade; this is called **interpreting**. Interpret changes in shape, size, range, quality, direction, weight transfer, and so on. Eliminate the opponent's potential advantage or use of force by adjusting your position to accommodate those probabilities. In evasion you must move from the center (every action, whether evading or delivering force, must be done literally from the center), be continuous in awareness and response, never let up attention on the activity, keep your feet under you (remain balanced and continuously free to move any- where), and maintain a calm mind. Beyond evasion there is the task of taking the initiative; this is always empowered by joining the movement of the opponent's body and intent before you touch (before contact). Lead his intent and action instead of merely evad- ing it. As he commits himself, use the shape and purpose of his action to destroy it; whatever takes form has its own weakness, its own end.

Taking the initiative

All actions should be timed. Evasion and leading will only work if the action of evading is timed relative to what the opponent is seeing and doing. When attacking it is essential to know the proper timing. Basic timings are: to attack before, during or after the opponent's action. To attack before his action requires the abil- ity to sense accurately his impending intent. An attack during or with his action must be timed to arise under the cover of his own commitment to act, thus making use of his inability to change and the likelihood that his attention will be on his own movement. To attack after his action is to follow his movement as it tries to complete itself, and make use of his lack of freedom from the process in which he is still engaged. Follow his actions and attack as if moving in between the waves. Another possibility in timing is to attack where he is not: where his attention, action, sensitivity, level of consciousness, sight or perception is not taking place, or is not up to meeting your attack.

In order to act appropriately one must be able to maintain mobility and change through "stepping" adjustments. Every step has a two-fold purpose: to evade and to attack. The two-fold purpose is realized by accommodating his action and accomplishing your own advantageous action in the same movement, all the while remaining centered and free to change again. Remember that response to activity should be from an impulse into the feet and center. Beyond this, develop the ability to direct different parts of the body to meet various events in various areas of the body in many ways, simultaneously.

Delivering force

In brief, any attack needs to have an effective and appropriate amount of power behind it. Although speed can be overcome and is not the only or even the most important factor, it nevertheless creates an advantage and must be understood and respected. Just so, power or delivering force is necessary in combat. Without it one must eventually lose, no matter how good he is in other areas. Few understand how to use force effectively (most don't even know this since they are never called upon to test it); they know neither how to receive it, nor can they make the distinctions necessary to adjust to what is forceful and what is not.

There are many kinds of force. I will briefly outline the components behind the intrinsic force that I use. Essentially, the mechanics I have already discussed are the study of effortless power. Hand-up-you-down is a primary ingredient, as is maintaining a firm and balanced connection with the ground through one foot. Aligning the whole body takes practice, so that at impact (in striking) or upon compression (in uprooting or throwing), the body and all its parts fall into the right place to allow for compression from hand to foot to occur. The force should be delivered *from the movement alone*. In striking, for example, your job is done *before* impact, so that as the force is delivered you are simply following through and completing the movement. If force is not delivered simply by allowing the process to complete itself while you relax and follow the movement, then you have not done your job— which is primarily set-up and alignment.

Make sure that the hand (or operative body part) arrives before the body movement as a whole is completed. Use the whole body to put the hand in place and also to follow it into the target. Don't move the body mass and then try to force the hand to the target afterwards. The center must have at least a small movement left after contact. This occurs when everything has fallen into place, so compression can naturally occur. Many factors are required for effective and effortless power, but very few people really understand what these are. You should learn what delivering force is about, and the various kinds of force human beings can access, so that you can recognize them in an opponent as well as use them yourself.

Huan Sheng—"the ontology of boxing"

Huan sheng means "To spring up on every side as prolific as thought." Essentially, *huan sheng* is creating a context in which the phenomena of time and space, as well as every aspect of objective relationship, are experienced as open possibility in this moment, and in such a way that our activity is continuously and openly appropriate to the changing event.

The event of being as it appears in the psycho-physical and metaphysical is the field in which *huan sheng* takes place. Understanding the laws or foundation principles that govern our thinking, perceptions, actions and reactions is absolutely necessary, since this art is simply establishing an appropriate relationship to these unfolding principles. Although much of the event appears to be beyond the realm of conceptualization, our relationship to it is conceptual, occurring in a dimension that most people call experience. That which is beyond concept for us may only be another dimension of concept, simply an unthought or unthinkable one. It doesn't really matter, since concept is simply a function of Being and Being itself is non-conceptual. The power of this statement, however, lies in experiencing what concept actually is, which is, in itself, a non-conceptual event.

Although the field to which I'm referring is far too immense to discuss in detail here, I want to make some points and open up some possibilities for you.

A BRIEF LOOK

In order to be effective, the concept of any movement or relationship that you want to express must be whole and real; whether it comes as an image or a feeling, it must include the whole body-mind and the currently-experienced relational condition. Then the form of action or expression can be consciously created in relationship to the actual and occurring event. The best expression comes when no attempt is made to hide the ego-structure, and it is either laid out or laid to rest.

Beyond ego

In taking on such a ridiculous task as freeing our self from our self, we need to experience and grasp our own reactivity and tendency, and develop action and relationship arising within the possibility that is non-reactive and non-tendency. For this we need to create a relationship to a possibility outside of tendency. To the force of our tendencies this will probably look like giving up, letting go or surrendering. There are many dynamics to which we need to surrender. We need to surrender to obtaining no credit or acknowledgement, thus surrendering to not winning or losing— the overwhelming tendency is the desire to win (others' love, respect, approval, etc., and not lose the same). Therefore, surrendering to disgrace or humiliation is often worse than the fear of injury or pain. We need to look beyond our own concerns, to see the whole event, to watch the other, not just the self. Our attention is bound so tightly to our personal concerns, worries, fears, goals, desires, and viewpoint that it is truly rare to notice or experience outside of that arena. Yet we must allow experience that is completely free from personal concerns, in order to take action within the possibility of non-tendency, which represents for us the possibility of the event itself and so the possibility of establishing an appropriate relationship to the event.

The tendency is to show our own concerns and demands by using strength or "forcing" the situation, thus trying to force into place what we want, regardless of its appropriateness to the event. It is necessary to surrender to the principles of process, to the event as it is occurring in this moment, and to the proper timing of our actions.

Do not indulge in fear (which is always of a future event and the possibility of being hurt); or in pain (an interpretation of the event in which we say we are being hurt); or in anger (which arises in relation to a past event, such as upon having been hurt).

Shifting beyond being stuck in our exclusive side of the matter—our personal concerns, tendencies and reactivity—is fundamentally necessary to do this work.

On Intention:

Your intention must be clear and free from attachment and design (pure, so to speak), so that the opponent cannot sense your intentions and move before you, and so that you can "see" clearly and move before him. Be empty with no demanding thought or idea of your own to interfere with your attention on his intention. Also, if you have any sense of doing something wrong to another you may be bound by your own nature to damage yourself or undermine your success, due to what you hold is evil intent. It is not necessary to have evil intent to relate effectively even in a fighting context.

Such is the case in methods like those of *huan sheng*: it is the "idea" that is enacted and made real through feeling-awareness (the force of being alive) and understanding. Detach your mind from any thought of outcome when acting. Use the life force to fill the body and, with no-thought, act. Maintain non-action and harmony of concept, body and energy. Use the spontaneous response of Being through the life force as **disembodied activity**. Develop great intuitive insight into right timing, non-separative actions, and turning the apparent scales—as in "who's doing it now?"

A Few Possibilities:

With the power to read another's "mind" you can see his desire, intent, fear, strategy, and framework. In this way you can use his own aggression to **lead** his mind and energy. Lead his action and even reaction in a way that is advantageous for you. Of course, you need to know that you are the target, the bait; feel this and use it.

From moment to moment, what will arise is what can arise

out of the functional design, the intent, and the experience/perception of the opponent in this very instant. Knowing this you can adjust accordingly and **eliminate his potential** for effective action against you. Develop an intuitive feeling of this dynamic and allow it to adjust your actions. Then you will never be where he wants or expects you to be. Out of the ability to "read" him, you will gain the capacity to **"start after and arrive before,"** which is to say, to see his intent to act, and handle it before he can bring it to pass. Know his intention to move; be inside his mind, move when he has any attachment (to form, idea, emotion, etc.). Take advantage, like an eagle hovering to strike, or a cat to pounce. Remember, even a fake fakes something, so adjust accordingly and move; take advantage of the action that is there regardless of its design. Be engulfing and overbearing, and maintain the advantage; stay full, and allow no gaps in space or time. Understand that all actions fill space and leave space; and in human beings, a "mind" directs that act. Compliment, follow, or borrow the energy of that mind.

When **following**, attack between the waves and into his contraction. Whatever action arises from the opponent, be it conceptual or objective, we can **borrow** the energy and movement of that action to adjust or create our own, like riding a wave to surf. As he uses force we join him, and cycle or spring that force back onto him. Keep an intent to move towards him, no demand on how, simply folding-in like flowing water. Relax the shoulder and hip joints of the limbs that are involved. We can borrow his energy, like a force field, and without contact use it to push our body around. Like water, we need only one inch to fill any hole in his defense.

Whenever someone has made a choice this means he has no **choice.** He can only choose what he chooses from moment to moment. Once we see his "choice" we can act accordingly, and he can't resist. Any action creates holes; when he chooses the action we choose the holes. These holes, however, are not static but changing in motion, and there are many kinds of holes. Confused or distracted feeling-attention pulls away from where it would naturally be, leaving holes. Learn to sense or "see" holes in his perception or in his field of awareness, and thus create the capacity to *do that which he cannot detect, or can do nothing about.*

Combine and interchange all of the methods of *huan sheng.*

Change to the appropriate action from moment to moment, so quickly, so subtly, so smoothly, and so continuously, that he cannot comprehend your actions.

A simple look at internal boxing:

1. Develop a **willingness to experience:** no avoidance of or resistance to the present. 2. Keep a **continuous open awareness:** listening, interpreting, outreaching and joining the event in every moment with your feeling-attention. 3. Any action taken must adhere to the principle of **following** or **joining:** follow and join activity, intent, impulse, and action. 4. **Creating:** conscious, intuitively intelligent and appropriate expression in harmony with what is, in truth.

The warrior's task: without concern, play the game as it is in this moment. No winning or losing—simply the fulfillment of a task.

Chapter Eight

In Conclusion

T here is so much more to say about Cheng Hsin and about
this teaching consideration that I could easily write four or
five more volumes without having to repeat myself. However, I couldn't do it without implying, referring to, or coming
from the fundamental principles outlined in this work. As a matter
of fact, much of what is stated in this book is a doorway to deeper
levels of the same thing, or to other possibilities of Being and
Reality. So from here, with work and contemplation, you could
reach all of the teaching.

I'd like to mention some of the implications inherent in this
communication, and touch upon some things that have not been
discussed. A word or phrase will be all I'll say about something
that deserves its own volume. These brief considerations will at
least provide for you a direction and the possibility of a new opening. After all, Cheng Hsin is you, and I've not said anything that
isn't already true of you.

The question of confusion

Total workability is inherent in the way things are. One of the
main dynamics that keeps us from realizing that workability is
confusion. We confuse one thing "with" or "as" another. We
"fuse-with" (con-fuse) many things on many levels. In other
words, we fail to make necessary distinctions, and so regard two
things as one, or something other than the thing itself as the thing
itself. We fuse thoughts or feelings, with that which they are a
thought or feeling of; and we fuse by association—mental, emo-

tional, physical or psychic. Often we fuse Being with what appears
as a self. We need to deconfuse what is what and produce clarity
and workability. This is usually called mastery.

Confusion, as an individual activity that is expressed in a
form such as "I am confused," often arises to cover up and ignore
or negate the fear of being controlled. Fusing things from the past
or present into one, meshing moments and events into the same
event, makes the moment indistinguishable and thus not handle-
able. What it takes to handle an event lies in experiencing the
necessary distinctions and "reality" of the event in every moment.
Fusing moments is an active avoidance of what's so, often motivated by an unwillingness to experience the possibility (or fact)
that we are controlled by this event or another being, that we do
not feel capable of handling. Denying the situation by not participating is being confused, and so not experiencing the truth or
the moment. Also, this is one of the ways the mind tries to hide
that which we consider weak or inadequate in ourselves. The fear
of being controlled arises from the sense of having no true ability
to survive (no direct capacity for life). We deny the event or "game"
so that we will not encounter the fact that we are indeed being
controlled. Reactive confusion appears to the self as an alternative
to facing the presence of what, in some form, seems to us to be
loss or death.

> *Instead of focusing on the accomplishment—the 'wisdom'—*
> *focus on the ignorance.*

For our motivations and "pursuits" to become clear to us, it
is necessary to understand the dynamics and principles in which
they exist. Some points to consider: We find that fear is the force
of ignorance (avoidance) and that an *unwillingness to experience* is
the foundation principle of fear. Increasing consciousness
decreases fear. Increasing feeling-attention decreases the "need"
for fear. Anger frequently arises as a result of not taking responsibility for what is or may be, which arises out of the same principle
that founds fear—an unwillingness to experience. The phenomenon called pain or hurt is a distinction that indicates the context
in which the principle that manifests as an unwillingness to experience arises. Pain does not exist as itself; it is an interpretation. The
context for pain is the same as for preference. However, since all
of this is fundamental to our beingness it cannot truly be grasped

without directly experiencing the very nature and ontology of self. This requires serious contemplation.

Within the resistance *to the event is the link between separation from it and 'union' with it*

Increasing attention, intuitive consciousness, and the willingness to experience anything (foolishness, being wrong, loss, death, etc.) runs counter to this tendency toward confusion and avoidance. Trying to fight the negative cycle (sluggishness, fear, reactiveness, avoidance, etc.) is a battle you must eventually lose. *You* will have a hard time overcoming it since *you* are doing it. You must see the choice or decision to do so, and thus realize that it is your very framework that must be dropped. In a pursuit of some sort, this often looks like letting go of winning and losing. You must change the state of being, for you cannot change radically within the same state; change the context, not the content.

We are not 'less' (inadequate, incomplete) and in need of additions to do 'better'; what we need is to simply be with what is

More protection feeds fear; have 'nothing to protect.'

Look into your own case. Are you mostly reactive, responsive, or withdrawn? What is the nature of relational condition? What "affects" it, or influences it, from moment to moment? Is there such a thing as cause? Investigate the possibilities called time and space, and the relationship things and beings have with each other, on every level, from subtle to gross. Look to see the obvious as well as the not-so-obvious (which is often simply the obvious uncovered). Look into the face of the unknown, which is what you see before you right now!

Continue to discover what "process" *is*. Understand that result *is* only process, and bring process and result into the same moment, the same place and event. See how you participate in the whole condition. You find it, allow for it, adjust to it, set it up, but you don't make it! You don't "do" the result. You participate in the condition, a condition which supercedes what you identify as you. You grasp the process that produces a result and participate in actualizing that process. Notice that all you do or participate in produces a result, even if it is not the one you think you want. To understand what creates a result, you must clarify what is what; you must deconfuse all that has been confused.

Another word about intrinsic nature

I suggest that we want to use the intrinsic qualities or power in our body and being; but rarely do people actually grasp that "intrinsic" means already there, inherent, and that nothing need be done about it! We don't develop what is intrinsic. We don't have to do anything to bring it about. It already is. It takes no effort to let something be. Simply use it as is, don't strain.

We can notice that all things have an intrinsic nature. This intrinsic nature is not found by looking beyond them or outside of them. It's found in the thing itself existing as the thing itself, without confusion. That which neither comes nor goes in a thing is intrinsic to it. Energy has its intrinsic quality, as does body, ground, floor, interpretation, table, and concept. Even that which comes and goes has an intrinsic nature and force to it, such as a thought or feeling; as does that in which it comes and goes, and that which produces the coming and going.

If we've confused things, we will have difficulty in experiencing the intrinsic quality in either of the things we've fused together. Since we're not dealing with the thing itself, its intrinsic power will not only be difficult to perceive, but difficult to use.

For example, when we tap into one of the intrinsic qualities of wood, it burns. Now, if we've confused water and wood and have a waterlogged piece of wood, we will have a very difficult time getting it to burn, because we don't know the difference between water and wood! It is the nature of water that it doesn't burn well. On the other hand, when we light the fire with wood only, it doesn't take any effort to have it burn. All of the intrinsic power released or used is simply a result of our participation in the condition that would have that be so.

Expanding upon the analogy, let's consider a match. The match works because it is "set up" to tap the intrinsic qualities of the items involved. When we strike it, we actualize the burning of the match by participating in the condition that draws upon those intrinsic qualities. No effort is needed, only the energy it takes to set up the condition. Notice that no matter how hard we squeeze the match, or what we think or say, or how angry or nice we get, it doesn't light that match! There's nothing we can do to make it burn. We can only set it up so that it does what it does naturally. If we do any more than that, that's confusion.

I would like to direct our attention to the fact that the very Condition has an intrinsic nature. The "base" of existence, the nature of all things, what *is* regardless of what comes or goes on any level, is called Absolute. It is the Absolute Intrinsic Nature. It is also called T'ai Chi or Undifferentiated-Absolute. That which allows something to be intrinsic, the source and nature of everything, is called Wu Chi or Absolutely Nothing! It's intrinsic nature is *not*. It has no quality whatsoever. It is not relative, and therefore is called ungraspable. And these two, Absolute Condition and Absolute Nothing, are *not* two. They are not even one, since one implies the other. They are not different, nor are they separate. This is called Paradox.

Reality: a concept, perhaps?

Within the self that we are (that which is identical to our culture), there is little or no room for not knowing. This is unfortunate, because when we recognize the basic truth of the root condition, we find that we are indeed that which *is* not-knowing and not-known (absolute formlessness, the "knowing" of which is formed); that abides in a condition that is referred to as Absolute Being; and an activity or natural function of unconditional participation. We are "being" that which is not knowing, yet fully participating. To the "knower" that we strive to be this presents quite a dilemma, one that we feel a strong need or impulse to resolve.

A manipulative approach to life (doing, seeking, avoiding, involving oneself in the events to attain or avoid something, attachment to the form of things) will never change it. No matter what is done, figured out, manipulated, accomplished, subtly or grossly on any level, it will always remain the same, since that *is* the event. No resolution is possible; it will never be "solved." "Not-knowing" has no impulse or demand. It has nothing, no win or lose; so nothing must be done.

We need to take a look at the possibility of some fundamental confusions on which this dilemma is founded. Confusion is possible in that *NOW* is an absolute, and can appear as or "be" both one way and its opposite. "Being" appears in this place of *now;* therefore, it can appear as separate and as all there is, as inside and outside of time, and as incomplete when there is nothing missing.

History as a whole is equivalent to the form of this moment. Within the phenomenon of time, the existence of form in this moment is seen as all that has come before it. This moment records, so to speak, every moment of form that has occurred prior to what appears to "be" now, much as a house *is* the form of every moment of building it to its completion.

Existence is arising in every moment, since form must always arise from no-form. In a sense, form "sits" in a base of no-form, as we "sit in" or "come from" a base of not-knowing. Since this event in form appears to us as all prior events in form, there appears to be a continuity to existence (time), and this existence appears to be the root condition or real, in that it seems to have meaning and necessity in itself. Similarly, we feel that as an individual we have meaning only in relationship to all we have "been," and that our nature is altered in this moment by an act in the last. This is not true.

The attempt to become complete by manipulating the form is already founded on a sense of being incomplete, and thus already incapable of accomplishing that task. Yet we seem to have no choice in the matter; we are driven both to survive as we are and to try to become whole and "known." From this position we create affectations in order to manipulate and "be." As we struggle in the arena of manipulation it appears that our choice is either to overcome or to surrender to others. From this we abuse or are abused. Realize, moreover, that to allow others to abuse us is to abuse them. We nevertheless desire to be truly creative, yet don't really know how to go about it.

If there is a form which we feel we must adhere to, plug into or arrange in any way to be powerful or manifest creativity, and we "do" that, then we are pretending or affecting power and creativity. On the other hand, when we are being powerful and creative, that is where we're coming from and so no form is considered. Not being separate from it we cannot view it since we are it; and form arises out of being, quite incidental to our condition. Then we are being powerful and creative, the source of which does not lie in form.

Of course, much of what appears as the state of our present body-being is an aberration, or adaptations that arose out of a limited and manipulative relationship to what appeared to be so at the time. The body traps or holds (is affected by) emotions and mental movements because the body feels, and emotions are felt, and our body does not discriminate between "feelings." One of our never-ending tasks is to free up the body-mind from the over-whelming number of adaptations that we have adopted and assumed. Most of these live in our conclusions and assumptions, and the principles on which they are founded. These make up what we call reality, or the way things are. None is true in itself.

We can understand the dynamics involved in the event of being alive, yet "enlightenment," or direct experience of the nature of Being, is necessary to see beyond dynamics and form, and so create the possibility of recognizing the source of dynamics or "dynamic" of dynamics.

A breakthrough experience of the nature of Being may occur in any moment that arises without form, meaning or design. Such a moment reveals to us our actual condition, and changes our relationship to all that appears to be, showing it all to be unnecessary and inherently meaningless. This provides for us the possibility of real creativity. Besides providing freedom and insight, the value of such "enlightenment" is to reveal to us the source, and therefore the course, so that we may properly and consciously align our own event to meet the demands of being alive. This requires nurture and discipline. So even when we "enter disturbed water we can still align with the moon," until such time when we can look at it directly.

The principle behind the principles

The Cheng Hsin Body-Being, which includes the principles of its function, implies something very personal about you and me. It represents a "way" of being, and this implies a source that is inclusive of all that we call reality, since the way of being at which we are looking must be totally functional in, and in alignment with, reality and our relationship to all things. The source of this way of being is the source of psycho-physical existence. It is the source of *you*. It is the meaning of Cheng Hsin. Cheng Hsin itself is the Source of Being. It is Being that is not different from Reality.

There is no room, not one inch, that is not already complete, nor is independent or separate in any way. Our mistake is to think that there is.

It must be understood then that the Source of all "things" cannot be a "thing." Neither can it exist in or as time and space, since these are limitations and principles within which things can appear. Nor can it have any form, or emptiness of form (which is a form also). It must be absolutely no thing and not separate from anything, or different from anything, since if it is separate or different, then it must be some thing. So the nature of the Source (Cheng Hsin) is absolutely paradoxical; still, it can be directly "experienced."

What we want to do, then, is move closer to the source of the event. Therefore, it is what we stop doing or don't do that is the center of the principles of Cheng Hsin, which give birth to the teaching of Cheng Hsin. It is only our habitual base of doing, our constant activity, be it psychic, mental, emotional or physical, that make it appear that not-doing is an activity, an effort, or a "doing" itself.

Calm is simply the state of being that is when nothing is "done" with the activity of interpretation to create uncalm. It is the same with **relaxing, unity, grounding, centering,** and so on. This "un-doing" of the habit, though, is quite a practice and so founds this "way" of being. It is uncovering what is already so.

As we return to that which is free, simple, and intrinsic; that which is nothing and not occupied; is open and not filled; then creating becomes marvelous and appropriate and powerful. Struggle lies in the doing and resistance to doing, not in the free participation in, and creation of, being alive.

We should notice that there are "events" which are actually "non-events." They simply appear conceptually as events. Most of what I've mentioned are the non-events, such as the principles. An example of a non-event is **presence.** Presence is not something we do, but is seen as such. It is what is so when we stop creating that which is not present. You see, presence is a function of being now, and since there is no other time than now, you can *only* "be" now. So presence is not something we do; being now is what is true, and we don't have to "do" what is already true. Presence, therefore, is not what we do to be here; it's what we stop doing to not be here or ignore being here, now. **Integrity** on all levels is not something we do either. It is just so when we stop lying and segmenting and creating splits in our Being, our identity, and our relationship to things.

This point on what's not-done, or the non-events, deserves further contemplation. The fundamental principle that seems to emerge in our consideration here is Nothing. Not a negative, not a removal, not an absence, nor an exclusion of anything; simply and absolutely Nothing, inclusive of all that is and of the very heart of Being. Consider it.

In this work, my idea has been to thrust a spear direct to the core, since mere scratching at the surface is basically useless; furthermore, I wish to allow a foundation of understanding to become clear and useful. Although there is much more to say about Cheng Hsin, and many profound and equally basic principles to be discovered and distinctions to be made, nothing is more practical nor more useful than what has been presented so far.

In completing my communication to you in this book, I feel both very honored and humbled. Within these pages, in my experience, are represented some of the most powerful experiences available to human beings. However, the operative word here is "represented." All of this is only a symbolic representation of the experience or truth of what's being said; and a "doorway" to much greater or deeper levels of the very experience first touched. If, upon opening this representation to experience, you are not excited, you're not blown away, you do not experience greater capability, fullness, and aliveness; then I suggest that you did not experience or understand the communication. If this is ever the case with you at any point in relationship to this text, please go back and actually experience what's being said. This may take your own investigation and inquiry outside of any considerations presented here.

If I've managed to play even a small part in your experience of *This* and of your own event, I've accomplished my purpose in writing this book. For this I truly thank you.

An Interview with Peter Ralston
January 1979

The following material began as an interview for a magazine article and became a rather in-depth probe into the heart and history of Cheng Hsin and Peter Ralston. It was recorded in 1978 in the course of several meetings and hours of discussion. It is conversational and presented as such. It deals mostly with historical matters involving the purpose and founding of Cheng Hsin, and the experiences that allowed and served Ralston in discovering and formulating the Cheng Hsin teachings.

Excerpts have been taken and used elsewhere, but the bulk of this interview was never presented. The material used in the forward for this book will not be repeated here. Because the information it contains seems worthwhile, it has been presented for the value you can get out of being a part of these conversations.

Q: What martial arts do you practice and what is the fundamental basis of them? Speak as if people don't know anything about martial arts except what they've seen on "Kung Fu."

PR: You want to make it hard? (laughter) Basically any time I speak it has to be like that, unfortunately. It is difficult to address myself to people who know nothing about Cheng Hsin because for such a long time I separated all of my study and training from other people; I separated myself even from people's common understanding of martial art, and so there's a very big gap. If you want to bridge it in a moment, or even in a few years, it's difficult. So one of the things I'm working on now is how I can communicate it more effectively.

What I do is Cheng Hsin. Cheng Hsin is the name of the communication that I put out. It's also the name of the school.

Cheng Hsin translates in the neighborhood of "Your True Nature," or "Integrity of Being." *Cheng* means "principle," "true," "genuine," "sincere," that kind of thing. *Hsin* is often used in Zen and Taoist terminology, and one of the main translations is "Heart," meaning "Being," or "the essential nature" of something. So Cheng Hsin is the Source of Being. What I do is communicate that, and I have lots of "forms" in which I do it. I have studied a lot of martial arts. In this school, I teach three internal systems of martial art, but we do so much more.

Q: What is the difference between an internal system and an external system?

PR: An internal system is a real study of martial art, or of psycho-physical interaction. It concentrates on fundamental, natural principles that are mostly overlooked in other pursuits. For example, an internal system has inherent in it relaxing the whole body, using the whole body all at once, deriving power from the ground, intrinsic strength, the use of ch'i or energy circulation throughout the body and that cultivation; breathing, the psychology of the whole matter, perceptive skills, developing this area (points below his navel).

An external system, on the other hand, is just a training of the body. A few centuries ago, an internal martial artist stated: "An external system is something you can learn by observation alone," by watching somebody. I can move and show you an external system. An internal system, I can't.

Q: Can you apply an internal system to an external system?

PR: Not necessarily, no. You can apply a lot of the internal principles to any body movent and incorporate that perhaps, but you see, the principles of external systems are different—for example, if you don't relax you can't generate certain kinds of power. Without sinking you couldn't come from the ground. You wouldn't be using your whole body; you'd be using individual limbs, like your arm instead of your center. This would not be an internal art.

Q: What do you mean by "coming from the ground?"

PR: Generating the power of movement from the ground. We relax and sink; sinking is a very important part in an internal system. To sink: the word *chen* in Chinese also means "to perish"—I always liked that, "to perish"—and it also translates "to sink." We sink attention, weight, energy, mind and ego, and everything else, down. Drop it down into the feet and down into the ground, so that the center is lower in the body.

When I do this I feel very much lower in the body; it feels like my observation moves down below the navel, and my strength and motivation fall down into my feet so I can stay very relaxed. I may hit with my hand, but the strength and power of it comes from the foot, not from the hand. I don't do anything with the hand; the hand is relaxed and the strength comes from the ground. Circulating the energy throughout, I align and unify the body and create movement aligned to my purpose. The whole body moves together. The strength and power of it come from the floor, not from the hand. It is simply a matter of getting the ground that I am standing on to manifest in my hands.

We make a connection between the ground and hand through our whole body. There has to be that connection, and it must include the whole body's movement, pressures, energies, and attention, all aligned to end up compressing into the foot and ground. By moving our body and circulating the energy from the ground it comes out the hand, simply through the movement of energy, intention, and purpose. But it is not like the hand or arm has its own strength, it's just hanging out.

Q: You are a channel for it.

PR: Yes. It's like a copper wire and electricity. The wire doesn't do anything—it just sits there and lets the electricity go through. Or like billiard balls when they're all set up in a line; you hit the first one and the last one goes. Those connections must be made, otherwise it won't work.

People will comment now and again that when I push them, or when they run into me and bounce off, that it feels like a wall. Or I'll hit them and they feel that in my hand. But it didn't look hard, it didn't look like much ado; it looked soft, but I touch them and still there's some force to it that they often interpret as a wall. I'll say: "The reason you think of it as a wall is because it is. It's just the one that is lying down." You see? The floor is very much like a wall, but we don't relate to running into the floor; we relate to running into a vertical wall, and that's what they're feeling. They're feeling the floor in my hands, in my body. They're getting the floor because I'm on the floor sinking down and allowing my body to compress into the floor and so the energy of the floor is transferred to the body.

Q: So you give the qualities of the floor a vertical form?

PR: Yes, that's part of it, but there is a lot more. We actually penetrate beneath the floor, meaning that our energy goes beneath the floor. And to give the qualities of the floor a vertical form is more than just penetrating beneath the floor. For example: Here we have the floor and we're standing on it. OK? Your perception of the room right now has in it: up, out there, to the left, right, and that way, and to the floor, you see? Most of the time people go around with their perception of the world having more "up" in it than it does down because we are always on the ground, you see?

Q: Right; it's a visual barrier.

PR: Yes. A visual and then a mental one, because we don't conceptualize, we don't even just allow that space goes beyond the floor. Think about that, right? That space actually penetrates in that direction (pointing down).

Q: An unexamined assumption of life.

PR: So, naturally, having that assumption, you'll walk around and the energy of your body and perception will tend to move up and out in your search for the world, in your observation of world, your relationship to that, much more than it will down, and that throws the balance off, you see? That keeps you up here. And thinking a lot. The balance is not correct. So, for real functional purpose, just to balance that, we have to include as much down as we do up. We have to include the concept, the experience, the energy, of the fact that space goes down.

Just balancing the energy of the being, the life force, to radiate in all directions is good; and then, to take on the specific demands that are involved with body movement and function, we need to form a real connection with the planet.

There is a mass which is this planet and it is really heavy. In fact, it is the biggest "heavy" around. If you want an ally, that's certainly one to have, because it is the biggest one. So, we have a little body, sitting on this big planet; making a connection with the planet gives us access to the power of the planet. This takes into consideration more than perception. In this we are considering functioning with the psycho-physical forces involved in interaction.

Therefore, we want to drop the center of mass, *the* fundamental point for any movement, and maintain balance and body activity. So we perish by dropping our prideful structure, but still maintain the body. The idea is to bring the center of mass and our sense of being down to the feet. Whereas the center of mass and our sense of being is usually much higher. What that does is bring the center of observation down to the lower belly, and the center of mass and motivation down to the feet, and that's a very high level.

Q: It sounds like you are assuming on a physical level that the source of power is the center of earth.

PR: Our greatest relationship, as far as masses go, is with the earth. That is the most attractive mass around, that's why we are all hanging onto it!

Q: (laughter) We're stuck to it.

PR: Yes, we're stuck to it, and so you see, external systems, for example, don't tend to notice that, whereas an internal system does. Well, in Cheng Hsin anyway, because most internal systems—perhaps simply out of the nature of systems—I believe are missing the point; I mean pursuits that are calling themselves internal systems. You have to realize that what I'm saying is not held or even known by all internal arts.

Q: How original is your work?

PR: In some sense, very original, and in some sense not so original. I learned a lot from my teachers. If it weren't for my teachers I would not have moved into some very important observations and considerations. They opened up a lot of areas for me, taught me, and assisted me in breaking through a lot of stuff. And what I do is still quite different.

Q: So, how unique is your school and your teaching?

PR: Very unique; there is none other like it.

Q: Is it a synthesis?

PR: It's *not* a synthesis, it's a discovery. Sometimes people talk about eclecticism, and I'm not eclectic. It is not like I've pulled from here and there and the other thing. I didn't do that. Cheng Hsin is at once discovered and created. I discovered it and in so discovering I also created it. The first manual I wrote started off saying something like: "Cheng Hsin is perfect already. It's perfect not because I made it perfect, or anybody else *made* it perfect, or because it was *made*; it is perfect because it is just what it is. It's what *is* Being!" It's not a system of my beliefs, it's not something I made up, it's not my fantasy, or anybody else's, you see? I looked and it was there. I have nothing to do with it. But that's very unique. You see, most people don't truly look. So when I did, an incredible communication I call Cheng Hsin came up. It was both created and found. It is at the same time the way that it is, most fundamentally, and what is merely occurring as a function of Being.

Q: So the name Cheng Hsin is entirely yours? Why would you, did you, choose the oriental, the Asian words? Because of its accuracy technically, or why? Why didn't you call it Ralstonizing or something?

PR: (laughter) One reason is because of the accuracy, because I couldn't find a word that I could say it with. I've started to use Integrity of Being, but when I say that do you see what happens? People hear what they think. Being translates from *Hsin*, which means your nature, your true nature; it means Consciousness itself, the origin of mind and heart; where mental activity, conscious awareness, heart, feelings and even life force, all come from. But when I say Integrity of Being, whatever people relate to is what they will get. When I say Cheng Hsin, nobody knows what it means, and that's true!

Q: Then they have to find out! That's very interesting. So, really you are starting a whole school, a whole system?

PR: That is something I resist; like saying that I'm doing something like Aikido or T'ai Chi. Somebody started T'ai Chi and somebody started Aikido, but I resist that.

Q: It's like you hesitate to claim ownership to something that you can't own.

PR: Absolutely. The thing is that if I said: "All right people, here we have Cheng Hsin. It's a whole new system. It's founded on true principles, etc." First of all, people would say: "Oh, another one?" Right? They'd write it off. Anybody can come up with a new system, and that's really useless. It's the difference between an intelligent mental facility creating more form, and the function of revealing what is true. There is a big difference. Making something up is not the same as revealing something that is true, understanding something, you see? And almost all systems now, even if they were true in the beginning, are just the form or shell of what was. In one minute I could make you a form, even a system. I could teach you forever new forms, new movements, new fantasies, new concepts and ideas . . . you know . . . the form of it, and then we could call that a system. Yet it's all worthless. It's not anything that has to be passed down from person to person.

In my opinion, what has become so for every martial art in the world, for the most part, is just that. It is just the form. It's not because people are evil, or because they don't want it; it's because, in essence, no form ever existed. So the only thing that can be passed down in existence through form is form. And unless somebody has a recurring understanding through that passage, or simultaneous to that passage, of the thing that's not formed, it is not going to be there. So, what 99% of the people get as T'ai Chi, for example, is the form. This doesn't happen only to the traditions, it also occurs in people's attempts to create something new and clever. It's usually an avoidance, an ignorance, and a function of an individual's egoic attempts to be creative without any real responsibility in the matter, and within the bounds of their own limitations and intelligence.

I don't want Cheng Hsin to be something that, in another generation will be, "Well, I do Cheng Hsin, and it *looks* like this."

Q: So how are you going to prevent this?

PR: I'm not. There's nothing I can do about that. All I can do is simply say what I've just said and teach it, and that's all. It's just not something that's going to be a form. I was telling you about the opening statement in the first Cheng Hsin Manual. Well, here it is:

> The principles of Cheng Hsin are not a random occurrence nor a system of beliefs. I was at the root of their creation. I have experienced them, so naturally I wouldn't look at them in this way. Yet, they were not made out of mine or anyone else's imagination. I looked and they were there. You may benefit from my efforts and experience, but only if you set out to experience them for yourself. They represent what is natural, what is true, and what is absolute. In fact, they have nothing to do with me or anyone else. Although I learned them and many great masters of the past expounded them, they are not mine nor theirs. I follow them because they are true; acting only as a vehicle.
>
> I urge you with all my heart to set out, free from any idea or demands, to find for yourself what is true. You must discover them for yourself or you will not discover them at all! If in giving yourself to experiencing these principles you find them not to be true, then do not follow them under any circumstances. But they are.

Q: What is the Cheng Hsin Body-Being, precisely?

PR: That's when everything is complete, everything is handled in the structure of the body, everything is conscious. The body-being is structured in alignment with the principles of mechanics and function that found the design of the body-being. Holding and moving the body, energy, and attention in alignment with these principles. The integrity and inclusion of all that is present as a multi-dimensional event of Being for the purpose of being effortlessly functional and fully awake.

Q: Define ch'i for me.

PR: _____ .

Q: That's it? I got it. Would you say something about it?

PR: It's life force. The force of your life. Now, that force is not specifically heat, or tingling, or vibration, or anything else. It's not specifically those things that sometimes manifest with the movement of feeling-attention. People will play with energy flow and get things like that—heat and tingling, and shaking and heaviness in the blood. What that is is the life force moving through and activating one of the senses, thus producing some manifestation. Energy itself is formless. It has relationship to time and space, but it is formless in the relationship. It doesn't have any rigid structure at all. It has no boundary in particular. However, it appears as an area of concentration, it can concentrate, but it has no definite boundaries, you see. Formless sort of like air is formless, yet not some "thing" that is. Therefore, it can take many forms.

It can be directed by your attention. So what you do with your mental activity, crazy or not, affects your life force. If you're going crazy with some sort of interpretation, your life force gets crazy and your body and your life become upset.

One of the things about it that people don't see is that it is not seeable. You affect your life force in your life with the crazy things you do with your thoughts and feelings, but it's not like you always see that right away. It's not like when you go crazy you get a flash of heat over here, or something as clear as that. But it does disturb your life force. Your mental activity actually is a manifestation of the life force, you see? That's why I say "Consciousness" when referring to *Hsin* as opposed to "mind": because your thoughts, your feelings are all movement of the life force. That is simply activity or movement of the life force.

Q: The mind itself?

PR: Yes, all of that. Do you see what I'm saying? "Mind" and life force are simply a distinction in the same event. People tend to confuse the effects of something with the thing itself. For example: when you are moving your hand or increasing the energy flow through your hand using an act of attention and conceptual direction, some things might begin happening to your hand. It might start getting warm. It may start tingling, start buzzing, or whatever. That's not the energy . . . people mistake that: "Oh, it's the ch'i. Ch'i is hot." That is the result of the energy or feeling-attention moving. The life force channeled like that touches the nervous system and creates tingling; moves the blood and creates heat, moves the energy to concentrate and the blood collects and makes it heavy; goes into the muscular tissue and starts to make it go a little crazy, and so it starts to vibrate or shake. That's the way that I hold what happens. That the energy touches stuff on the way through.

Q: It's just a symptom, a side effect.

PR: Yes, but if it weren't for little things like that people would have nothing to relate to. I'd also like to say that it can appear as paradoxical. It doesn't adhere to the physical or objective rationality, the way we're used to solid things adhering to normal physical laws, so it seems paradoxical. For example, I may sink energy *en masse*, my whole sense of being . . . literally, the sense of being me . . . massively moves down. And it feels like I go into the ground. My whole sense of being goes down. All of it. Now see, this is the paradox: I can act with my whole sense or force of being, my energy, my feeling-attention, and still leave it all down. I raise my hand up and hit you, for example, from down there. All of it connects up to hit you, but none of it leaves, you see?

Q: Yes, I think so. It doesn't behave like I think karate or something would that's just physical, where you would lose force by exerting yourself through those principles. And through this you're not exerting yourself, but just being a channel for it.

PR: Yes. Also, when you do internal systems with the right teacher and the right development, at some level you develop power such that when somebody hits you, it doesn't hurt. That's a result of internal training.

Q: You mean they physically hit you and it doesn't hurt?

PR: Yes. It doesn't hurt because you become . . . like rubber. They hit the body, the thing, and because the life force or energy has built up after awhile, through a specific training, perhaps it fuses the tissue and makes it like rubber, and permeates the bones and they become like finely tempered steel. The body energy doesn't resist and it also doesn't break.

Another seemingly paradoxical endeavor is that of conscious attention. You want to put absolute attention on your partner or opponent and, at the same time, you want to put 100% attention on yourself, your energy, the body, and the direction of those. And you have to do 100% of both. It sounds paradoxical, but it isn't. It isn't only when you realize that the two of you are one event. When you see both yourself and your opponent as one event, then your concerns are not limited or restricted to this side or that side. You simply have 100% attention on the whole thing.

Q: I'm really getting the complete difference of this approach. It's like learning how to fly instead of playing basketball or something. Their similarity is only that they both occur in life.

PR: The difference is actually greater than that. True, it would be hard to make a comparison, but it's like what I said in one of my handouts, the difference is that Cheng Hsin is a real and open study of what's going on, the event that we are, an investigation of Being. Other studies are not even close. At best they're a piece of it. I have the hardest time communicating just what it is I do . . . the ballpark. How to tell somebody easily, communicate to somebody in a few paragraphs, even in a few days, what this is about. Just the immensity, the different levels, approaches, the value, and all of the things I could go into that it is all about, is hard to communicate. Beyond that it is very difficult to communicate that which I can't talk about, the understanding. See, when I'm sitting by myself I can have an understanding like that (snaps fingers). For example, all of a sudden I can see how something works, the principle out of which it functions, or see how something can work, but I can't communicate it because the imagery or the understanding of what I got is not common, you see? It is not something people share. If I have an understanding about an experience of the nature of Being, it is extremely difficult for me to communicate it, because others are usually not coming from the same understanding, the same experience. They have nothing to relate to. So my work is largely creating environments in which I can communicate this work. It's my new endeavor and it's not an easy task. However, it should be so simple, so obvious, that I should be able to say, "look," and it would be apparent. I feel that it should be that way. It's so simple!

It seems to take a great deal of time for people to understand Cheng Hsin. I'd like to shorten that a little. (laughter) It seems to me if I could be more effective in my communication, I could set it up for people to get the experience more readily. They would really hear what I'm saying and use it. If I could be more effective at that there would be a shorter period of time that it takes them to get it. Also, I want to make it more powerful, to have them get it more deeply. Even before someone's fully grasped it, I can still deal with them on the level of an experience of Being. I can still talk to that, and on some level they'll get it no matter what, even if they don't consciously click into it in the moment. I try to do that. Then again, there are the people like the grocer at the corner store who is simply an open, conscious person who loves life and lives life. That's beautiful. I really don't have much to communicate to him. You see?

To me, I could just sit here and experience Cheng Hsin. I don't have to do anything with it. It doesn't have to be in any kind of form, you see? That's why I don't like to say what I do is simply martial arts.

I've found a lot of joy in this work. I've experienced a lot of joy. I almost break down and cry for joy sometimes. Once I was doing a routine and it was feeling perfect without any thought of its perfection. The tremendousness of that *******! There is a beauty that I can't really talk about; a tremendous, great, beautiful thing happening, and I was just feeling it. When I stepped out of the movement I didn't think about it, I simply felt gratitude in my heart, love and gratitude and I wanted to thank somebody. I turned around, and there was nobody to thank. So, I bowed. My body just went down. I bowed as if my body and heart just wanted to express a deep respect and gratitude for no "reason."

Q: Tell me what you think about this: Fighting, almost axiomatically, refers to an adversary relationship and what I get about Cheng Hsin fighting is that you are working to not be in an adversary relationship, and that other forms of fighting are based on an adversary relationship. So, the thing about Cheng Hsin is that the more you master it, the more you transcend the adversarial quality of relationship, the more you do that, the more there is no fight, and the less you would create that in your life. In other words, Cheng Hsin gets to a point where it transcends itself, you might say, or perhaps not itself, but the whole business of fighting. In fact, it's about the opposite, which is fulfilling relationship. What do you think about that?

PR: That's absolutely true. The point is not to have a problem, but an opening. The game we play looks like fighting. It is fighting for awhile, but, like you said, Cheng Hsin study transcends itself. I think anything that is worth pursuing, is something that will transcend itself. If it's something that just keeps turning around and around in itself, it is not worth pursuing.

Q: Does it transcend itself, or just the form?

PR: The form. You have an idea of fighting, and you have an idea of Cheng Hsin that will change continuously. The purpose for studying anything changes continuously. Like I say, everybody who walks through the door has a different reason in their heads why they are going to be here. Usually what draws them is a desire to add something to their ego, or make-up in limitation, but what draws them to stay is something else. Because people will leave right away who aren't drawn to what is worth staying here for. Health, physical exercise, staying fit, learning how to fight, learning self-defense are all side effects to the study here, not the purpose.

This is a study of Being. Not just a fascination or mystic fantasy, or self defense. People usually begin thinking they are studying some little thing. Learning a fascination, and involving themselves in a fascination, in a mystic internal martial art from China, self defense, or learning how to dance. If nothing else, it is very healthy to the mind and the body to get touched and to have a situation where you're playing with somebody, like a child, and relaxing and just moving bodies together; feeling, getting touched, and touching, even when the contact is a game of fighting. Yet that is still not the purpose of Cheng Hsin.

Mechanically, you could look at fighting as having an opponent. But an adversary is something that you are fighting against. In other words, someone with whom you have a conflict of interest and, in this case, a physical conflict of interest. They are going to hurt you and you have to hurt them and/or you have to "do" or "be" in such a way that it is anti-them. You see? The attitude is "anti-them." Whatever they are doing, whatever they are thinking, or feeling, you have to do anti-that. You have to destroy that;

be an antithesis of that. Separate from that. The bottom line of most relationships is to be protected from it. To not be anti-that is to be part of it; it is to be part of them, and move with them, and not against them. Then you are not fighting them.

Q: But you could still hurt them.

PR: Sure you could. But you are not fighting them. The purpose of Cheng Hsin fighting is to have a tool to look at what we are already doing; and then to understand and transcend it. To be able to blend with somebody physically, you have to blend with them mentally; your energy has to, your consciousness has to. You have to be able to be with them; and in order to be with them you have to be able to be with more than yourself. This offers an opportunity to do that. Perhaps the idea about being in life is to do the same thing, is to be with it rather than against it.

In any case, it looks to me like that would certainly make one happier. I'm happier when I'm being with life than when I'm fighting the world. I grew up fighting the world. That was my attitude, and so Cheng Hsin has turned me around. Learning to do this with just one other, another human, is difficult. Things that get in the way come up. And the things that get in the way here are the things that get in the way out there too . . . avoidance, resistance, fear and anger, and all that stuff. We look at it all, and see what it takes to do it and not to do it.

Q: OK. Now, I'm intrigued by everything that you just said, and the fact that you have demonstrated that you can choose to hurt somebody in that context. Like, you said . . . in the last match at the World Tournament . . . you had to hurt someone.

PR: You can choose to hurt somebody and it's like hitting a bag, for example. You are not really fighting the bag, you are hitting it. Do you know what I'm saying? On another level you could say that they will get hurt because they want that. They are engaged in that and if that is what their demand is, that is what they will produce. That is what will happen. They want an impact. They want some sudden, definitive contact, and you supply that. Sometimes people, I mean really, sometimes people who like to fight a lot want to get hit, for whatever is going on with them. They want to punish themselves, they just want to feel it, whatever. They want to get hit.

Q: So, what does putting your foot into someone's body have to do with consciousness and a transcendent view of life?

PR: Well . . . (laughter) . . . in a nutshell, violence is an aspect of the world and it is not something that is separate from the truth. I've seen people who view "truth" as something which is apart from other things, apart from the very raw quality of the world. Like truth is only light and love and floating around. And I don't choose to look at it in that way. What I consider truth to be is the truth. Avoiding the shitty, bad, violent, cruel things, or that which we label as such, is not to be *with* the world, is not to turn into the truth of it. To avoid it is not to transcend it. I don't think that anybody ever transcends violence by avoiding it, by walking away from difficulty. And by violence I mean to include emotional and mental violence, verbal violence, etcetera. All the stuff that we label as bad. I don't see that emotional violence is that much different than physical violence. You're hitting my emotions, you're hitting my body, or you're swinging at them. If I'm in the way, in either case, you'll hit them. And if I move them in either case, then you will miss. That is just your swing then.

If you look at Tibetan spirituality, apparent violence is very much a part of it. I like some of the things they say, just like I like Freejohn. He's very straight. There's no avoidance of any kind of relationship. Whether it looks like it is violent, whether it looks like it is loving, whatever. I mean people are going to fear sensuous exercises. They could have stuff going on about avoiding that. I have students who are very nervous about relaxing and yielding to someone, being touched or just playing. But like the Tibetan thing, the truth of the world is going to be very direct. Violence is very direct, if you are in relationship with it.

The object is not to experience pain in particular. The object is to be open to it, not to recoil from it. So, I'm going to put my foot in your body. Your objective, your movement, is to blend with that so there is nothing going on. There is no contradiction in our movement. To do that you have to be open to what that would be if there were contradiction, or the pain that would be created if there were contradiction. If you are not open to that, chances are you will freeze, or you will resist, and you won't be conscious enough to really blend with that continuously, again and again. You see?

The possibility of pain creates a level of fear which is very revealing about where we are really at with our ego. About where we are really at with the way we deal with the world. When you get into a lot of fear, things come up. It's like the bottom line. It is not just a lot of good intellectual ideas and nice philosophy. It's admitting: "That's where I'm really at with the world! I'm really afraid of it, no matter how much I talk a good line." Or whatever it's really like for you. You get to see that. Usually levels of intensity or the possibility of physical injury help to bring that out. Emotional intensity and the like help elicit that. Also, people need to make a distinction between what we could call ruthless facilitation and violence. A skillful facilitator or teacher may appear ruthlessly confrontational, producing a great deal of discomfort in a student. Although quite real, this is on purpose to serve and support the student in a breakthrough or to recognize something they would not recognize without such service.

Q: I get the intensity of it. It's not just violence it is intense and that brings up intense stuff. One of the things that I get from what you are saying is that a crucial factor in here is the context in which you are holding fighting, or your attitude about it. If what you are up to is beating up the other person, then you could do one action and it would have an adverse effect. But if what you are up to is playing or expanding your consciousness of what is, then you can do the very same action and it would support the other person. In other words, someone could put a foot into my body just with the intention of hurting me, and that would create an effect in the world. And a person could put their foot into my body with no particular intention at all. They could just be playing with me or being in relationship with me, fighting or something. Then, as you say, that would occur as a result of a hole in my consciousness or awareness, and it would be the very same hit, in the very same place, the very same action, but a completely different trip. Is that your point of view?

PR: Yes. That's quite true.

Q: OK. I'm curious. I have no idea what this question is going to bring up, but how sexual is fighting? I get the intensity of it. Sexuality is also something that gets to where people are at very, very fast. Do you have anything to say about that?

PR: They're very similar. A lot of confusion and avoidance arises in sexuality as it does in fighting. People have confusion about expressing it at all. Trying to keep it in, being sensual and getting nervous about that. Confusion of what feelings are about. Feeling somebody. Sometimes people don't want to feel somebody else because of the confusion of sexuality. All this stuff comes up, but it is simply feeling someones presence, you see? Not knowing what is going on, really, just that what you are doing is feeling their presence, and it doesn't mean anything sexually. I find for myself, personally, however, that they are very similar. They are both very satisfying. Once I had the thought: "If I'm not going to make love, I'd really like to be fighting." (laughter) I realized the connection I have with those two. That they are both very much the same for me in a sense, because in both I get contact. In both I have a relationship. You see? In both I have a very close, intimate, feeling and satisfying relationship. And they are both intense and they can both be a lot of fun. They are both an intimate play with somebody.

Q: What is fighting?

PR: One of the biggest breakthroughs in fighting occurred for me when I realized that: "There is no such thing as a fight, there never was and there never will be."

Q: So, what did you do with that?

PR: There wasn't anything to do with that.

Q: Well, what happened from that?

PR: I tried to get it across to people, but that was difficult, so I shut up about it.

PR/Q: (laughter)

PR: Now, I at least try to get them to play in relationship rather than by themselves.

Q: What do you mean by that?

PR: Well, very simply, here is an incident that exemplifies this: I was playing with someone and he was throwing punches and kicks and this and that, and all of a sudden he was about to throw a punch and so I stepped aside, but he threw it anyway. And I'm not there! I'm standing there, watching this happen, and he literally does the punch over there and I'm over here. I said to him at the time, "I'm over here." (laughter) "Why did you punch over there, when I'm over here?"

See, that was more than not perceiving that I had moved out of the way. He was more into what he was doing than what I was doing. People don't recognize that what they do is absolutely dependent on what the other person is doing.

Q: So, fighting is not about what you do, it's about what the other person does.

PR: Absolutely. And there is no fighting.

Q: And there is no fighting.

PR: You can't do anything except in relationship to what they're doing. Absolutely. Absolutely! If they stood there and let you hit them, you're still absolutely in relationship to what they're doing. And if they are moving around and doing what looks like fighting, you have to do everything, every movement, in relationship to every single moment—not the last moment or the moment before, or what it looks like they might be doing—but to what they're doing every single moment. Their movement, their change, their mind, their energy, their thoughts.

Q: So around the time when you were twenty years old, you really began contemplating the serious questions of life, out of which you had a number of enlightenment experiences. Do you think this helped you in your work?

PR: Yes. I think experiencing the nature of Being has helped immensely. Most people haven't had a direct experience of Being and can't readily lock onto that truth. That experience, whether or not it changed anything in my life directly, is responsible largely for my being able to detach myself from a point of view. It was knowing what I am that enabled me to see situations more clearly, so I could just give up my point of view, my demand. I think that's very valuable.

Q: One of the things about enlightenment I think people have the wrong idea about is the idea that enlightenment is the end, that the enlightenment experience and increase in consciousness is the end, and if they reach that—nobody actually says it, but there is a sort of implicit concept—that it is over. What I have noticed is that enlightenment is really a beginning.

PR: Yes I agree with you. It's not the end at all, and we do tend to look at it that way. People with a "spiritual gig" look at it that way. There are stories about the complete enlightenment finally reached, Gautama Buddha and all that. But holding it like that is not functional for our purposes. If it is complete, then it is complete in every way that you could think of it. Every facet and dimension is complete. What happens is somebody has an enlightenment experience that is absolute but not complete. Probably to the degree that it is not complete, it leaves you with a struggle of incorporating it into your life. An enlightenment experience, given that it is absolute, *is* the truth absolutely, but it may not be recognized as ultimate. To the degree that it is complete and in the areas that it is complete, or in the areas that you are complete or in alignment with, those areas disappear. Where there used to be a lot of activity that you "did" things about or worked on, and it was either a problem or an effort or even just a lot of attention and energy, such an experience can make that disappear, no longer be a struggle or a problem. It becomes clear and simple, not complex.

Yet, changing the way we are, deeply and as a whole, is a continuous and often a slow process. Realization or breakthroughs come suddenly sometimes, but is followed by a lot of realigning and transforming and tempering.

Q: It sounds like Cheng Hsin creates a foundation for direct experience to occur and be integrated.

PR: Yes, like Shissai said:

> When the Heart is motionless . . . Heart, again, is *Hsin*, or "Being"; he is referring to exactly the same character . . . *When the Heart is motionless, the life force is also motionless. Man's heart is not originally evil. If he allows himself to be guided by his true nature, and is not led astray by passions and desires, his spirit will be free from need and his responses towards things will be unhampered. Nevertheless, the errors of the Heart ensnared by passions are often most profound. One cannot simply exchange one's temperament and return it immediately to the simplicity of one's nature.*

Even after an enlightenment experience it is difficult to simply exchange one's temperament and return to the simplicity of one's nature. He is talking from the point of view of already knowing what one's nature is.

Part of it has a lot to do with the rearranging of the mechanics of things—like your body-being, your thinking, emotions, even perception and experience itself. Because you are going to operate as a body, and you are going to operate in relationship with all that can and will come up that you are associated with. To recognize what mind is, and to alter your relationship to that activity. To recognize the stuff that you do that you always thought was done to you, and so straighten that out. You realize that there is a choice. Recognizing the state of assumptions that you are in that is not serving you allows freedom from them. And you can recognize these things when you are doing something like fighting. It's a psycho-physical relationship, so the whole event of "being you" is involved, and it equates with all that you do. Noticing that, and changing it by getting an opportunity to experience what it is, and noticing how that really changes your state.

One thing I say to people about relaxing, for example: "If it feels the same as before, it probably is." If I say: "Completely relax your tissues and move around in a very deep state of relaxation," and you say: "But it feels exactly the same; I don't notice anything different." Then I would say: "If it feels the same, it probably is." When you relax completely it feels different from when you don't relax, and you get an opportunity to notice that. When you change your state by surrendering to the activity that's going on, then you feel differently, you act differently, you even perceive differently. But sometimes it is very hard to perceive what that shift is. You see, it is not easy to identify. Like when you are playing with somebody, and you "try" to shift your state. That doesn't work. You try to give up something or experience something and it doesn't work, then it is real frustrating.

Q: In other words, you can't do it without doing it.

PR: Right. And, by and by, through practice, day after day, year after year, you begin to cultivate an appreciation for what that shift actually is. So that you can move into it much more quickly. You can do it.

Q: Okay. Now, with regard to enlightenment . . . I don't know if I'm making this up, or you actually think this and you just aren't saying it. My view on this is that enlightenment absolutely clarifies for a person their relationship with their body and their mind and the world . . . in other words, if you're identified with all this crap that you are not . . .

PR: It "de-identifies" all that, but I don't think it elucidates all that. You see, an enlightenment experience, before "complete enlightenment," can absolutely reveal what your true nature is; but what your true nature is is not found or grasped in the workings of mind, so it does not absolutely reveal all the intricate workings of mind, the patterns that you've set up since you were born, and maybe before.

Q: It makes apparent that that is all your mind instead of you.

PR: The question is open. The nature of what you're speaking about can't be divided into "sides." Enlightenment doesn't necessarily do that by itself. It takes another activity, one that appears as a process. It is within this event that we must find out what the event is, and then maybe we can change it, if that's appropriate. It tends to transform you or move you in that direction, and I think, depending on the "depth" of experience or breakthrough, it can simply clear things up. Things that are ready to fall away you can just throw out, but deeper things don't necessarily transform immediately, since you return to living life from basically the same habitual position.

Q: So, Cheng Hsin is a way to evolve your nature and to experience more of the truth.

PR: Cheng Hsin is Being; there is no "way." What is done at the school is to provide an opening for people, and so it looks like a way.

Q: So, it appears as a way to manifest your true nature and evolve this nature that we are associated with, the body and the mind, etc.?

PR: We could say that. Apparently there is an event taking place, it is the event that we "are" and "in which we find ourselves." It is the event of being. "Life" appears as an activity, a process, from the time we are born to the time we die. We live largely in what we call our mind; and it appears like it's something already there or set up. We have a body, and it is bent out of shape the way it is bent out of shape, or not. And we have the activity that we call our feelings and emotions. And all of that is plugged into the way that we relate to everybody and to life in general. Yet we don't really know what any of it is. Cheng Hsin is about not ignoring all that, but taking a look at it the way that it is, in a context of relationship with other people or simply in studying the event as it appears in a body-being.

Q: So, how does enlightenment relate to that?

PR: Enlightenment elucidates the nature of this event. By elucidating the nature of the event, it allows an alignment with it and freedom in relation to it. It frees the event of Being from these complications that seem to be necessary and fixed, so that you are not attached to them although you are involved with them. I find that changing one's temperament, which is one's relationship to the event, is a matter of freeing oneself from the attachment to conclusions and assumptions, what we generally call "knowing," which is a very strong attachment. And since we are still personally involved with it, we are attached to it in that way. Changing that does not happen in a moment, even though an enlightenment experience does.

Enlightenment puts interpretation and the usefulness of all that aside and leaves you with Being. However, in the process of being alive all of that stuff keeps coming up. A direct experience of your nature empowers you in putting it aside, or letting it be as it comes up. Once you experience the nature of the event, it is invaluable for working with the event. That in itself, however, does not work with the concerns and motivations that will continue to press you forward in this event. It is invaluable because it is the truth that founds being alive. And working in the truth is the only way to transform something. You can't transform something if you are not working with the way that it is. So, it is invaluable to have enlightenment experiences. It is also important to work with "this event" and to have a place to do that work, because an enlightenment experience does not completely transform the event. Like you said, it is a beginning, not an end.

Q: Is Cheng Hsin work dependent on the student having realized their true nature?

PR: No. You can begin work on the event of your life without knowing what Being is. You can transform your life without knowing that it is Being doing the transforming. It will probably take longer because a lot of energy will be wasted working on yourself not having a direct and authentic experience of what founds the work and you, and because you will have a more limited access to the unthinkable. Although people make progress studying only in the classes at this school, our intensive workshops are more powerfully directed toward a direct experiential penetration of what one must get in order to really move in this work. I notice that I have a lot of love for people in general, and I notice that I really have a lot of admiration and respect for people who are willing to do what is necessary to get to the truth.

One of the things about having an experience of Being is that it allows you to recognize your mind as a point of view and not as the truth. And that is invaluable and transformative. As long as you hold what you think as right, and not merely as a point of view, then you are stuck with it and it appears as real or the reflection of and assessment of reality. And it is not. You have to recognize first that you are not what you think, then freedom is possible.

Q: Literally and figuratively, that you are stuck in a point of view?

PR: Yes. So, I work with people on that level. Some people can not relate to what they think enlightenment is, but they will hang around this atmosphere, knowing that there is something here they want, long enough to open up to where they can become interested in this work. I've had people who have never had a major break-through specifically in "consciousness work," become much clearer on their nature and what is happening, and do work on transform-ing themselves without calling it that. It is most noticeable to people who have seen students of mine three or four years ago, when they come back and look at the same student. They often comment on this transformation. They comment on the solidity that they see has developed, or on some change from when they saw them last. I get to see it, but I'm always around. It's easier when you can see it suddenly, in contrast to years ago. I have seen people do work in various "schools," "paths," or organizations, all with different approaches, and although some drastic changes or jumps may occur from time to time, in some more than in others, in the long run nothing is more actually transforming than Cheng Hsin.

Q: While you were talking about your World Championship I had the same kind of sense: that a lot of people view World Cham-pionship—whether it is basketball or boxing or whatever—they view it as the end, a place to get to. And I really get from you that you see it as the beginning and as an opportunity and a doorway, and that your job or duty has now begun as a result of having attained that.

PR: Yes. I did it for that reason. First, I had to get people's attention before I could do anything with them. People have to come to me before I can work with them. My work is found primarily in what I consider to be incredibly powerful courses and workshops. For example, I have a course I call the "Mind Course." It has to do with the relationship we have to the event of being—of "mind," living, experience, knowing, perception, emotion, convictions, and so on—all that we are and live. In this course we look into all of that. We deal with recoil and fear. What is fear, what is that really? Not just fear, a name, or fear, a feeling, but really get into it to find out what it is and how it is created. All the tendencies and reactions that we have, and the habits of the mind and the psyche. In the Mind Course we use fear . . . you can't fool that, you know? You can't sit there and say: "Well, I'm going to be very calm and clear," when it is just scaring you to death! We use that and bring it up, and see what it really is, really open up to it. I think that is very valuable, very valuable. It's valuable to bring that kind of investigation and questioning into life. We generally hold things like they are what we think they are without ever noticing we *really* don't know *what* they are, nor have we truly looked into the matter deeply. This positioning profoundly gets in the way of being alive. The whole event that appears as Being is the undertaking of Cheng Hsin. Being grounded in this kind of work makes such an undertaking not only possible but accessible.

Q: Thank you.

Shissai's Woodcuttings

The following is an edited version of a discourse on the art of swordsmanship by Chozan Shissai, alternatively translated and freely rendered by Peter Ralston. This abridged version of wood cuttings written in 1728 by Shissai is the same as Cheng Hsin.

Preface

The use of the word "Heart" is a translation of the character *Hsin* as in Cheng Hsin, and can be read as "Being."

To get a sense of what *Hsin* is, we must look first to Being, then to the "Integrity of Being," which is a less accurate but more practical translation of Cheng Hsin. It's not that this translation isn't true; it is. It simply leaves more room for misinterpretation as it leaves room for usability.

However, *Hsin* is actually the source of being, so Heart refers to this source, as in "The heart of the matter," thus, the heart of being. This Heart, expressed many times by Shissai and myself, is not a "thing." It is not an "item" among the items of the world; it is the source of all items. The Heart arises into form (creates) via the life force, and so Shissai addresses understanding the Heart and exercising the Life Force.

Peter Ralston

Discourse on the Art of Swordsmanship

by Chozan Shissai

FOREWORD (Abridged)

If after a time one acquires the necessary physical abilities, the knowledge of how to adapt to changing situations, and faith in the body's movements, if one adjusts to the stillness or motion of a particular situation, recognizes one's own strengths and weaknesses as well as those of the opponent, and if one's thoughts and emotions are properly channeled, then one will come to know spontaneously the behavior to be manifested. It is only possible when emotion and intellect, hands and feet can meet the demands of the changing situation that a decision over life and death lies with oneself and not with the opponent. Thus, the following dissertation by Chozan Shissai is a discussion on the care of the Heart and the Life Force.

SECTION I

Man is a creature of movement. If he does not move in goodness, he will of necessity move in non-goodness. If a thought does not arise from the realm of one, then it will arise from that of the other. Man will never succeed in comprehending his Heart (Being) and, thus, in directly following the Divine Laws of his nature, if in his Heart and through his great strength of mind, he does not attain mastery in his studies. Thus I went to the mountains and overheard a master and his students speak. One of the students spoke:

The Principle is without form. Its function derives from the instrument. Without the instrument the Principle is unrecognizable. Although swordsmanship is directed toward victory and defeat, when one attains its essence one recognizes that this essence is the marvelous simplicity of the Heart (Being) in self-

149

revelation. The novice, of course, is hardly able to penetrate these realms overnight. Thus, the instruction follows the natural development of form, and so everything proceeds with ease and without strain.

One improves the harmony between bone and muscle, practicing hand and footwork, becoming prepared to meet the demands of every situation. If a person does not practice, though his heart may be strong, he will fail to fulfill his function. Form is practiced by a means of the life Force. The Life Force is that which defines the form by means of the Heart. One must, therefore, keep the Life Force lively and uninhibited, strong and balanced. By comprehending the Principle inherent in the technique, one conforms to the nature of the instrument. From mastery of action follows the harmony and balance of the Life Force; the action's inherent Principle reveals itself of its own accord. When it is understood in one's Heart and no longer generates doubts then action and principle converge, the Life Force is concentrated, the spirit calmed, and responses follow unhampered. If the actions have not been mastered, then the Life Force will not be harmonious and balanced, the appropriate form will not ensue, heart and form become two separate entities, and, therefore, one will not attain liberation.

Still another student said:

Now the form follows the Life Force, and the Life Force follows the Heart. If the Heart is motionless, then the Life Force will be motionless as well. If the Heart is peaceful and undisturbed, then the Life Force will also be harmonious and follow the Heart in this and very naturally do justice to the activity. Yet if there are irritations in the Heart, then the Life Force will be inhibited, and the hands and feet will not perform their function properly. Too much attention to technique inhibits the Life Force and causes it to lose its harmony and balance.

He who attempts to meet his opponent while waiting, concerned only for his own safety, develops into what is called a hesitater. He does not correctly understand what it means to "wait during attack and attack while waiting," and therefore takes refuge in his intellect and deals himself great harm. There are many who, while attempting to wait here and do their techniques there, are kept in check by an unskilled but strong opponent, forced into a position of defense and do not manage to take control, and fall simply because they have taken refuge in their intellect.

That unskilled opponent neither knows how he should react nor has a closed mind. He does not wait and does not hold himself back; he does not pause to reflect. His Life Force and Heart are equally uninhibited. Although his Life Force is clouded, his Heart unenlightened, and his method crude, he is still able to keep in check one who retreats into his intellect and has concern for his technique because such a one has thus separated himself from direct relationship.

True function is the natural response of the Heart, in retreat without form and in approach without a trace. That which possesses form and structure is not the wondrous unfolding of the simplicity of the Heart. As soon as the slightest refuge is taken in thoughts, the Life Force assumes form, and the opponent defeats that which has thus gained form.

If the Heart is free of irritations, then the Life Force is harmonious and peaceful, and when the life force is harmonious and peaceful, then it is lively and moves freely and is without rigid form· without using strength, it is naturally strong. The Heart is thus like water: as soon as intellect and thoughts disturb the Heart in the slightest, its clarity is destroyed, and it cannot unfold freely. Thus, one must know what it means to respond freely and without inhibition from the stillness of the Heart. Even though the Heart may be strong, if the form is not appropriate, then activity will arise where it should not arise.

As it is with archery it must be so: The will is firm, the form is correct, the Life Force fills the entire body and is lively, the nature of the bow is not violated, the bow and archer form a unity. When the bow is drawn, and the archer is completely with this action as the spirit fills heaven and earth, then the spirit is calm, nothing moves the thoughts, and the arrow is released spontaneously. After the shot, the archer is the same as before. If the archer's spirit blends into a union with bow and arrow, then the bow is also filled with this spirit and is an equally marvelous creature. If the bow is forcibly bent then the nature of the bow is violated, bow and archer oppose and contradict one another and there is no mutual permeation of their spirits. Instead the strength of the bow is inhibited, and is robbed of its power, and when that happens the arrow will not fulfill its function.

It is the same in everyday dealings with men. If the Life Force does not fill the body, then the latter will develop illnesses within; the Heart will atrophy, a person will be fearful within and outwardly inhibited, and he will lose the ability to recognize sublime relationships. If a person severs himself from things and is not in harmony with them, then conflict will develop. If the spirit is not calm, many doubts will arise and the person will remain indecisive about himself. If the thoughts are agitated, then the inner being will not be balanced, and this person will make mistakes in his life.

When the Heart is motionless, the Life Force is also motionless. To say that one's action is natural is merely to say that its principle derives from the natural potentials of the body and is directed towards its goal. Man's Heart is not originally evil. If he allows himself to be guided by his Nature and is not led astray by passions and desires, then his spirit will be free from need and his responses towards things will be unhampered. Nevertheless, the errors of the Heart ensnared by passions are most often very profound; one cannot simply exchange one's temperament and return it immediately to the simplicity of one's Nature. Thus, it is important to teach men how to acquire discretion, great insight, forthright convictions and an honest Heart; to teach them to acquire personal awareness and self-discipline, and thereby to place them on the solid ground of practice.

If one forgets life in the face of an opponent, forgets death, forgets the enemy, forgets oneself, if one's thoughts are motionless and one is free from the disturbances of the mind, and if one surrenders spontaneously to the natural flow of one's feelings, then one will be free in every changing situation and uninhibited in one's responses. Even though form may disintegrate to dust when one is surrounded by numerous opponents, and one may disperse one's actions to the right and the left and forward and back, not even the slightest fluctuation will appear because the Life Force is balanced and the spirit still. However, as my teacher said:

> *The error lies in mistaking inanity for an empty*
> *Heart and perceiving sluggishness as harmony.*

To use the technique "destroy with violence" is to drive down one's opponent from the strength and buoyancy of one's Life Force. It is imperative that one rush unerringly at the central power of his opponent. However, if a person does not know the advantages of form, then he will make mistakes. If Heart and Life Force do not build a unity, then a person will not be capable of an overwhelming burst of unerring energy that drives down the opponent. If, from the beginning of study, theory is the only consideration, then the student will lack, and despite all efforts, will never attain perfection.

And then the Master spoke:

Technique is to be practiced, confusing things resolved, mastery in actions attained, and one's essence and Principle comprehended. In this way deep inner awareness is attained. The master first teaches form without wasting a word about its significance; he simply waits for the student to discover this himself. This is called drawing but not shooting. Not because he is wicked does he withhold explanation. He does it simply because he wants the student to attain mastery through practice and the involvement of his Heart.

> *If I draw one corner, and he cannot transfer it to the other three,*
> *I do not repeat it.*

Thus the Master takes the student by the hand and pulls him on, it is no more than that!

If the Heart is too deeply involved in technique this will bind the Life Force, and it will not be harmonious and balanced. One might say that this is like forgetting the beginning in search for the end. Yet it is also wrong to totally discard practice and say that it is unnecessary. The function of swordsmanship lies in activity and form. If its function is discarded, what reference shall the Principle of its essence have? By practicing its function, one becomes aware of its essence, and it is in this awareness that the liberation of the function lies. Essence and function have one origin. There is no disparity between outward appearance and substance. Of course, sudden awareness of the principle is possible, but if technique has not been mastered, the Life Force becomes rigid and the form unfree. Action springs from the Principle; formlessness reigns over that which is formed. Thus, technique is practiced from the Life Force and the Life Force is exercised from the Heart. That is the order in which things occur.

If a person is mature in this art, if his Heart has penetrated it and he has proven himself in action, if a person is no longer doubtful or fearful, then his Life Force will be lively and his spirit calm; he will respond to every change in situation freely and without inhibition. Yet the knowledge of this grows directly from the exercise of, as well as trust in, the Life Force. Therefore, words only serve to help us explain it. That natural, spontaneous propriety of response, in retreat without form and in approach without a trace, its wondrous unfolding and unfathomable character, cannot be acquired simply by hearing about it from others. The Master's involvement is limited to pointing the student in the proper direction. That is not easy to explain, and therefore rare in this world.

Swordsmanship is basically the exercising of the Life Force, and therefore, at the beginning of study the Life Force is exercised by means of form. It makes no sense to exercise the Life Force separately from form, for then there is nothing upon which to test it. When the discipline of the Life Force has attained maturity, then one can proceed to the Heart. The wondrous unfolding of the Heart is easy to comprehend, yet it is difficult to retain freedom in every changing situation by means of one's own awareness. Swordsmanship is an art which is concerned with life and death. It is easy to give up life and die, yet it is difficult not to perceive life and death as a duality.

One asked:

If that is the way things are, then can a spiritual aspirant who moves to overcome the concepts of life and death attain liberation as it is defined by the art of swordsmanship?

He answered:

The goal of the exercise is different. This one hates the cycle of rebirth and lives in anticipation of his total extinction. He has estranged himself from life and death by binding his heart to death from the beginning. Therefore, when he finds himself surrounded by several opponents, even if form should turn to dust, he will immediately render his thoughts motionless. However, he rejects the demands of life. The only thing that he does not do is hate death. But to say that life and death form a unity for this one is different from our attitude. To surrender to life while alive and to death at dying is not to divide the Heart. Fulfill its way by following what is just! In this way does one attain liberation.

One asked:

It is one point of view to confront life and death without preference or aversion. Yet, when a person rejects the demands of life, does he not act freely?

He replied:

From the beginning, he turns his Heart elsewhere. Total extinction is the most important thing for that person. The demands of life do not interest him; for him only death is possible. For precisely this reason, he does not succeed in freeing himself from the demands of life. Life and death should not be perceived as a duality. In life one fulfills the Way of life and in death one fulfills the Way of death. Mind is not stirred in the slightest and the thoughts are motionless. Therefore, one is free in life and free in death. In contrast, that other person sees nothing but illusion and deception in the creation; nothing but dream and pretense in the world of man. And thus he believes that to fulfill the Way of life means to cling to life and to suffocate in its activities.

One asked:

But what about the fact that since ancient times swordsmen have joined with Zen monks and have learned their most profound secrets?

He answered:

Only when the heart is balanced will a person be able to measure up to things completely. On the other hand, a person will suffer from life if he desires it and clings to it. If a person is roused and agitated in all the fibers of his Heart then it only shows that his relationship to life is wrong. Those people of whom you speak had turned their wills to this art for many years, indulging in no rest, exerting their Life Force and mastering the technique; yet, the Heart had not opened in victory and defeat. They spent years and months being angry and indignant. Then they joined with a Zen monk and were taught the Principle of life and death. When they heard that all things of this world are merely transfigurations of the Heart, their Hearts opened up immediately and their spirits were calm. They released themselves from their former goals and thus became free. They had created the prerequisites for that act by having exerted their Life Force for many years and proving themselves in activity. He who has not yet matured in this way may follow the famous and wise teachings but he will still not gain enlightenment!

SECTION II

The Life Force is the origin of life. If the Life Force detaches itself from its form, then death occurs. Life and Death are simply fluctuations of this Life Force. If one understands the origin of life, then one also knows the ultimate meaning of death. If it is in life in which I presently find myself, then I am free in it. If it is in death, then I am also free in it. If one disciplines the Life Force, knowledge of the Heart will come of its own accord.

Although the principle of life and death is easily recognized, to worry about it even fleetingly is to have an Errant Heart. Since this Errant Heart moves arbitrarily, the spirit agonizes and does not know that it carries a great burden around with it.

The way cannot be seen nor heard. What can be seen and heard of it are merely its traces. The ability to recognize what lies behind the traces is called intuition. If learning is not intuitive comprehension, then it is useless. Take what I say with a grain of salt and do not take it literally!

Thus: It is the Life Force that determines form by means of the Heart. Therefore, the functions of the entire body are completely regulated by the Life Force. The non-material portion of the Life Force is called the Heart. It bears the divine Principle within it and is superior to this Life Force. Originally, the Heart is without form or sound, without color or scent, it acquires function only by means of the Life Force. That which penetrates the higher and lower realms is the Life Force. Every thought, no matter how insignificant, falls within the province of the Life Force.

The movement of the Heart which is caused by its encounter with things is called emotion. The transiency of observations is called thought. If the Heart moves in accordance with its perceptions and follows the Divine Laws of its nature, then illumination will pervade all of its activity and the Life Force will not move arbitrarily. To use an example: It is like a boat which, following the current, is driven downstream. Although it is moving, the boat is nevertheless completely still and shows no trace of movement. That is called being "motionless in motion." Ordinary men are constantly experiencing happiness or rage, joy or grief. They are continually driven by false emotions and thoughts, and thus are foolish and as if filled with dirty water. The slightest movement of a single thought is sufficient, that which lies in darkness arises and passions and drives are thrown into great confusion, and one's self overwhelms the Conscience. It is like a boat toiling against the flood. The waves rise high, the boat is in motion, one is inwardly restless. When the Life Force is in confused and wild motion, responses are not free. It is important to cut through the roots of one's illusions about life and death right at the outset of studies. A person must be persistent in order to recognize the Principle of life and death. He must discipline the Life Force, exert the Heart, and prove himself in the activity of combat.

When he has comprehended the Principle of life and death within his Heart, there will no longer be any doubts or mistakes. If thoughts are thereby rendered motionless, then the illumination will also extend into the Life Force; and it will be lively and agile and in turn take hold of the Heart, which will now act without inhibition or restriction. Then freely and without hindrance, the Heart will dictate the appropriate form. When the Heart obeys its feelings and its responses are quick, it is like the moonbeams which appear immediately when a door is opened, the tone that arises as soon as an object is struck.

The ability to respond is proven in combat. If one's self is free from thoughts, then the form offers no point of attack. If it does offer a point of attack, then it is the result of thoughts which manifest in form. If one's self is free from thoughts, this is called "having neither a self nor an opponent." If there is a self, then there is also an opponent. Since there is no self, then it is as though the good and evil, right and wrong of him who is encountered were reflected in a mirror down to his most minute thought. It is not reflected in one's self, it is simply a counter-reflection of whatever comes. Herein lies the marvel of naturalness. The desire to reflect another from one's self is a thought. And because this thought hinders the self, the Life Force is also inhibited and its responses are not free.

If one were to train with earth and heaven and all things in this world as one does with a sword, and were to destroy his limited and partial conceptualization of martial arts, then the whole wide world would be filled with light, and the responses of the Heart would be unhindered and free. Then, even if such powerful opponents such as wealth, nobility, poverty, low birth, misfortune and need, trouble and pain, were to close in on him from every direction, then his thoughts would not be moved even in the slightest, and these opponents would be repulsed as flies by a fan. When we reach that point, even without wings we will possess the freedom of flight.

It is difficult, however, to rid oneself of any particular thought to which one has clung from the very beginning. If he at least frees his Heart from the prison fashioned by selfishness, then nothing in the entire world will be able to set his self in motion, he will respond unhindered and freely. If only a single thought even slightly takes hold somewhere, then the Heart is trapped by itself. If the thought takes only a slight hold, then the Heart too is only slightly hindered. But if it takes hold strongly, then the Heart is severely hindered. Someone who has succeeded in mastering an art knows very well that a Heart ensnared by itself is detrimental to the practice of his art. Yet he will be incapable of relating to any greater context anything which he knows about the art's profound Principle which he has made servant to the art, if he remains trapped in it.

One asked:

What must one do then to advance one's study of the Way, to the practice of an art.

He answered:

The Heart is nothing but natural potential and feeling. The natural potential is the divine Principle of the Heart. It is still and motionless and possesses neither color nor form. It only becomes wrong or right, good or evil, through the movement of the emotions. If the mind no longer submits to tendencies and reactions motivated by preference and ignorance, and if the emotions follow the Heart, and if the Heart no longer clings to goodness and evil and is free from the stirrings of fear, then the mind will attain harmony and divine illumination, and intuitive knowledge will begin functioning. When that stage has been reached, then no trace of the mind will be found. We call that No Mind.

Yet, when the mind encourages feelings and desires, thereby resorting to manipulation and deception and does not maintain its totality in its various transformations, then the Heart is shackled and its illumination obstructed. This is called an Errant Heart. Since most people have made feelings and passions master of the Heart, they are held in perpetual motion by this Errant Heart and do not know what so plagues their spirit.

Direct Experience (Enlightenment) sweeps aside the mistakes

of the Errant Heart, the Heart's divine Principle is acknowledged and its light allowed to break through. Such a one is considered enlightened, and through recognition of the truth no longer resorts to the deceptions of the intellectual mind. He allows things to be things and no longer permits himself to be held fast by them. He immediately yields to events as they occur, has no desires, and does not hate. In life he submits to life and fulfills its way, and in death he submits to death and does not worry about what is to come. Although heaven and earth may change and move, it will not deflect his Heart; and though all things of this world may overlay it, that will not confuse his Heart. His thinking is not rigid nor his action dependent. If this is understood and its course followed and disciplined right from the beginning of study, then even idle chatter will become a means for exercising the Heart.

If in Swordsmanship one faces an opponent, he fences as best he is able and looks death cheerfully in the eye. What could then trouble that person? A warrior must only take care that his will remains unbroken, that the principles of his art are applied in his life, and that he recognizes his Heart in his daily activities. The ordinary man worries about heaven's deeds, but is negligent about his own. We cannot measure the deeds of heaven with our intellect. He is a fool who worries about the insufficiency of his intellect and thereby plagues his spirit!

If the Heart is not wrong, one will not inflict harm. Man's Heart is not originally evil, it is only that from the beginning of his life man continually uses wrongness to serve his development. By doing so, its odor permeates him without his knowledge. He inflicts harm upon his nature and is ensnared. When one recognizes the Truth and stills his mind, then he inflicts no more harm upon his inborn, original Being. Nothing more than that. If wrongness in the mind is only slightly avoided, the divine Principle will appear only partially. From the beginning of his study a person does not contemplate various thoughts, rather he behaves spontaneously and acquires technique naturally, and prevails over harshness with gentleness.

SECTION III

One asked:

What does it mean to be motionless in motion and in stillness, not still?

He answered:

Man is a creature of movement. Yet a man who possesses these characteristics may be very busy with his day-to-day activities but he does not allow his Heart to be set in motion by these things; his Heart is balanced and still, free from desire and not held captive by his self. If a man is confronted by a superior enemy force, even though he may dispense his actions to the right and to the left, his spirit will remain completely still in respect to life and death and his thoughts unmoved by the superior enemy's power. This is called "motionless in motion." When a person feels neither happiness nor anger, neither sadness nor joy, then his Heart is completely empty and troubled by absolutely nothing, it adapts to things out of this state of complete stillness and lack of desire, and masters the things. In this state, nothing limits his function. To be still and motionless, therein lies the Heart's identity. Its function lies in its being in motion. Its essence lies in its stillness, its claim to the principle of things, and its clarity. However, essence and function have one source. Its function lying in movement that arises from its essence which is stillness is "being not still in stillness."

When a warrior approaches an opponent, if in this act he is impartial, without hate or fear, without thinking "Should I do this or that?" and from this frame of mind adjusts to the approaching opponent, then that person's responses will be unhindered and free.

Although the form moves, the Heart does not lose its essence, which is stillness; and although the person is still, the Heart's function, which is movement, is not interfered with. That person is like a mirror, for he is still and without cloudiness and as he is exposed to the phenomena of this world, he reflects them in himself as they confront him and returns this reflection. Yet, when they have passed him by, he does not hold onto their image. The clarity of the Heart is of this nature. In times of motion the ordinary man is swept away by the motion, and thereby loses himself. In times of stillness he becomes sluggish and empty and does not do justice to his function.

What meaning has the image of the moon in the water? It is basically the comparison of the reflection of the moon in the water. There is a poem by the former emperor about the pond of Hirosawa that reads:

The moon casts its reflection unwittingly upon the waters which have no desire to hold it.

For the moon there is no gain or loss whether it is reflected in all water simultaneously or in none at all. One can comprehend here the wondrous action of the Heart. The essential thing, however, is that the moon possesses form and color, while the Heart does not. One resorts to the moon, which does possess form and color and is easily recognized, and uses it as an image for something which does not possess form and color. Of course, that is true of all images. In the search for meaning, however, one should not take examples literally!

One should have a tranquil Heart and no longer allow oneself to be overpowered by things. If the Heart is tranquil, then responses are clear. It is no different in daily life. Even if, as people say, the self were to plunge with a single bound into the depths of hell, it remains the original self. A warrior is involved wholeheartedly and does not hesitate. But should the Heart hesitate, thoughts will scatter as well. It simply means the Heart is not clear and that the person's actions do not spring from the whole Heart. Clarity grows from the motionlessness of the Heart and only then do the actions fly well-aimed toward a goal.

All these things are difficult to formulate in words. Yet it is highly dangerous for them to be incorrectly understood. A fundamental concern in warriorhood is simply to develop a lively Life Force and eradicate a dormant Life Force. Yet, if a person gives a name to something and then holds fast to that name, he will miss the real meaning. But if no name is given, then he floats about in empty space and does not attain awareness.

Weakness and suppleness are two different things. Suppleness denotes a lively Life Force and is effective. Weakness merely denotes a lack of strength and is ineffective. There is also a difference between tranquility and indolence. Tranquility is consistent with a Lively Force, but indolence is nearly the same as a dead Life Force. If a person is rigid, it is a result of the Life Force. If a person is quick in his technical responses and his Life Force is ready, then he is permeated with the positive and unhindered. A rigid Life Force means slow responses. There is a rigidity which develops out of the thinking process and one which develops out of the Life Force itself. Yet that which is called the thinking is the Life Force. What is known is called thought; what is unknown is called Life Force. That will be understood if it is recognized within oneself.

If one understands the Principles only in theory and has never experienced them physically through practice, then Life Force and Heart remain mere rumor and do not become realities. The awareness of the Heart of an adherent of swordsmanship who has disciplined his Life Force only insofar as it affects his responses in sword play will remain restricted to that single area. This person is unable to realize the potential which this awareness has for universal validity. When a person has grasped this essential meaning and affirmed it for himself, then it will benefit him even though he has not achieved technical mastery, because in doing so he has at least done justice to one side of the matter.

In many schools, teachers and students alike are led away from the door through which I believe they must enter. Consequently, they grow enamored with the landscape along their paths, and many stay there and consider it right. Thus, one sees them making a great uproar over the most insignificant educational theories and arguing among themselves over what is right and what is wrong. The landscapes along the way are merely appearances fashioned within the framework of the mind. As regards to the landscape, details could be discussed without end. The idea that "no one else knows what I know" is foolish. What is clear to me can be clear to other men as well. Therefore, it is superfluous to hide anything.

One asked:

Why use only the clearness and avoid the cloudiness?

He answered:

Fire and not water is used to dry something that is wet; that depends on function. A clouded Life Force is very heavy; a person is held fast in its sediment, thoughts remain stuck in it and err in its darkness and a person cannot free himself of that which sets him in motion. He is capable neither of self-determination nor of following other men; he is constantly anxious and never attains stillness—that is called being stupid. If a person recognizes the diversity of their effects but does not know that yin and yang have one source, then the Way is not yet clear to him. Likewise, if a person knows that they have one source but does not know that their effects are different, then he cannot yet practice the Way. However, should a person put his faith in heaven without having first fulfilled his human obligations, then he is not following the Divine Way.

A person cannot reach the Heart through words. All that he can do is regulate an excess or insufficiency in the movement of the emotions. Or, in the conscious awareness of his reactions, avoid the confused movement of selfish thoughts and bring himself to obey the Divine Laws of his own nature. How a person manages to do these things depends on the realization of his Intuitive Understanding. When a person's love shows itself in his actions, this is called having a conscience. If one trusts in one's Intuitive Understanding and follows it, and if one fosters one's conscience and does not bring harm to it through selfish thoughts, then the confused movement of a clouded Life Force can calm itself of its own accord and nothing will appear except the clarity of the Divine Principle. One need not follow any particular course in nurturing the Life Force as long as he has the firm will to do so.

One asked:

How is it that Buddhists denounce the intellect as something evil?

He answered:

The intellect is basically a function of consciousness and cannot be labeled as bad. It is only bad if it supports passions, withdraws from the original context, and becomes a person's main concern. If the intellect makes itself the main concern, if it supports feelings and desires and moves in a confused way, then even though a person knows that this is not right, he will find it difficult to bring his mind under control.

If at any time these matters are treated with secrecy, then it is done only for the sake of the beginner. If it is not done with secrecy, then the beginner has no trusting. Therefore, secrecy is inessential, it is not the heart of the matter. The beginner has no ability to discriminate; he understands incorrectly and, naturally, considers what he understands to be true. Therefore, it seems he is taught only those things that he can understand. If a person has penetrated to the heart of the matter, then he shows it to the beginner in detail and hides nothing. In Principle, there is no difference between the affairs of swordsmanship and worldly things. Once this is understood and the Principles practiced in daily life, if a student is fortunate enough to reach a stage where what is wrong can no longer defeat what is right, then that alone can be a great gain!

It is essential that the Heart be clear and unhindered. It is essential that the Life Force be strong and constant. Heart and Life Force are basically one. All the functions of the human body are called forth by the Life Force. A person whose Life Force is weak is susceptible and receptive to evil influences. There is a way for developing a strong and lively Life Force. If the Heart is not clear, the Life Force will stray from the Way and begin to move erratically. If the movement of the Life Force is confused, it will lose its dominance over strength and decisiveness and, through imperfect knowledge, block the light of the Heart. Though the Life Force of one's blood may be lively, a person's actions nevertheless will not be free if his Heart is in darkness. The Life Force of the blood is short-lived and without roots, and the results of its motion are ineffectual. From the very beginning, he who does not sweep aside imperfect knowledge and exert his superiority over the opponent, and who does not possess a temperament able to bring down a wall of iron, will not succeed in attaining mastery and penetrating to the essence of spontaneous behavior and naturalness. And because he inflicts harm upon his nature through imperfect knowledge, it becomes unsettled and weak and does not fulfill its function.

The Life Force determines the functions of the entire body by way of the Heart. Its essence consists of calmness of spirit, harmony of the Life Force, spontaneity of responses, and the natural pursuit of action. That should be examined and seen in one's own body. If a person simply reads it or hears it from another but does not prove it in his own body, then the Principle remains mere theory and does not become functional. If a person hears of the Principle, then examines all that he has heard in his own body and recognizes it in his Being, only then does he attain the perfect understanding of that which is right and wrong about things, that which is easy and that which is difficult. That is called practice.

SECTION IV

One asked:

In the art of the spear there are traditional methods of handling the straight spear, the spear with a crossed shape blade, the spear with a hooked shaped blade, the spear that is sheathed and still others. Which of these is the most advantageous?

He answered:

What a stupid question! It is the spear with which one thrusts. But what helps a person attain freedom in thrusting is his own self and not the weapon. Regardless of what a person uses in the beginning, relying upon the experience of those who have preceded him, he takes care to study and utilize all the advantages handed down to him, and thus attains freedom in usage. Yet, when he progresses and ultimately finds the way to himself, then even a cudgel becomes a spear in his hands. It may be a great mistake for a person to consider only the technique to be the essential thing and to think of nothing else. Despite that, however, a person must first and foremost master this knowledge. This is essential! If he misunderstands it, then he will fall victim to the mistakes of the beginner.

Inner cleanliness means to clean the Heart and free it from the dirt of selfish thoughts and unbridled fantasies; to return to one's true state of desirelessness and selfishlessness (Not-Knowing), and to nurture one's original, inborn, and heavenly nature. Outside and inside are basically one and the same. By circulating throughout the body, the Life Force allows the Heart to function. One must undertake first to dissolve the congestion in the Life Force and thereby still the Heart, to enliven the Life Force and thereby liberate the body.

Collect the confused and agitated Life Force and release this unbalanced Life Force and make it peaceful. Quiet the mind, relax the body, and circulate the Life Force freely and throughout. If one practices this daily, one will spontaneously experience a feeling of well-being. Out of this blissfulness, one will practice the art more and more intensively. If the Life Force is collected, it cannot fail to be enlivened. One will no longer suffer the misguidance of a sluggish Life Force. Since the Life Force fills the entire body, by even slightly enlivening the Heart, the Life Force is also enlivened.

Whether a person is singing, letting his voice ring out, is eating his rice, drinking his tea or walking along a road, if he continually strives to achieve this state, then in time it will become a permanent condition and he will enliven his Life Force in a thoroughly natural way. If a person suddenly remembers to practice this in the moment he takes up his weapon, he then can indeed renew his Life Force and rely upon his physical conditioning and technique to compose himself. Yet, because he behaves completely consciously when he does this, the Life Force is unsteady and irresolute and performs with difficulty when the person is confronted by the unexpected. Yet, if a person uses and exercises his Heart consistently, then he will spontaneously respond with propriety, even at the most crucial moment. A person must simply keep his Life Force lively at all times and not allow it to fall into sluggish ways. A dormant Life Force lacks its nonmaterial component. Thus, it does not perform its function properly, and, what is more, it often brings forth fear which causes a person to avoid things. On the other hand, if the Life Force fills the entire body and forms a living union with the Heart, then there is no fright, there is no fear, and a person can handle even a sudden change in the situation with ease.

When one draws the Life Force downwards and collects it in the lower portion of the body, after a short time it fills out and all of the inner spaces become strong. Fear and fight arise because the Life Force is gone from below and has settled in upper areas of the body. One can observe that ordinary people move the way they do because they have shifted their center of gravity upwards. A person who moves correctly has no movement above the hips. Because he moves with his legs, his body is quiet, his inner organs do not rub against one another, and his body does not tire. If the Life Force is unbalanced, he will not succeed in acting with his legs. By keeping ready the foot with which they will take their next step, they are free in the use of their feet. Thus, the Life Force flows back into itself and is not diverted by his opponent. He is collected and heavy in the lower parts of his body, and light above, and his movement is balanced. His voice resounds because he breathes from below the naval upwards. When he breathes, his stomach below his navel swells powerfully with air. Do not limit yourself to strategy! If a person continually directs his Heart towards all things in this world, he will share generously in its abundance. But the person who is foolish and empty is as good as dead. Things offer themselves to him, but he does not reach out to them.

A plan which runs counter to humaneness remains ineffectual, no matter how cleverly it was conceived. No matter how often a doctor may read his books nor how well he may know his cures, if he does not know the actual causes of the illness and simply dispenses his medicine at random, then instead of bringing about a cure, he will only create more illnesses. The knowledge of the warrior exists in his knowledge of humaneness. What warriors study today are the traces of the strategic art of famous men of the past, the dregs of the ancients. But a warrior is measured according to this: That he learns from the dregs of the ancients and extracts clear liquid from them.

In learning an art or game such as Go, there have been established moves since ancient times and, although it may appear that one can do no more than to learn them thoroughly, the master player is successful in arriving at new combinations not included in them. To imitate the established Go moves and copy the ancient chess combinations is to learn a plan. Yet once these have been learned, then the player develops additional new strategies from them and thereby decides the outcome of the game. If the situation demands, then the proper decisions will issue forth from the player's "empty" being.

By forever approaching all things with his Heart, a person makes everything which he sees and hears a means of exercising his Heart, and in an emergency he will be able to give himself completely to the situation at hand. He who does not know himself also does not know others. He whose Heart, trapped within itself, leads him to deceive and defeat another, will himself be struck down by his victim directly in the weak spot that is his Heart trapped within itself. He who attacks another out of greed will find his greed set in motion, and he will himself be struck down by his victim directly in the weak spot that is this motion. He who suppresses others through force will be struck down by those persons in the very spot where the force exhibits its inherent weakness. Only he who thoroughly knows himself and is free from the reactive tendencies and motivations of preference and ignorance is not vulnerable.

IN CONCLUSION

I have merely loved the art of swordsmanship since my youth. I have attempted to draw knowledge from its technique, examine the changes of my own Life Force and cure its weaknesses. I have heard about the Principle and striven for enlightenment of the Heart. And whenever, from time to time, I found agreement in my Heart, I recorded it, and only my youthful naivete has caused me to present it publicly. I sincerely beg of you to attribute it to my youthful naivete. I have put these words in the mouths of the mountain demons and thus made it seem that they were not to be taken seriously. How could I alone have ever claimed as the Truth a little volume entitled *Conversations Heard in a Dream?*

For More

If you would like more information on the work of Peter Ralston, including audio tapes, video tapes, other books, or workshop/study opportunities, please write or call us at:

Until December 1, 1995:
The Cheng Hsin School
6601 Telegraph Avenue
Oakland, California 94609
(510) 658-0802

After December 1, 1995:
Cheng Hsin
P.O. Box 11483
Hilo, Hawaii 96721

Please include your name, address, and phone numbers and whatever information it is you require. If you are writing a check to us for any reason, please make the check payable to Peter Ralston.